What The Brochures
Don't Tell You

WHAT THE BROCHURES DON'T TELL YOU

About Cruise Vacations

Tina Rinaldi

iUniverse, Inc.

New York Lincoln Shanghai

What The Brochures Don't Tell You

About Cruise Vacations

iUniverse books may be ordered through booksellers or by contacting:

iUniverse
2021 Pine Lake Road, Suite 100
Lincoln, NE 68512
www.iuniverse.com
1-800-Authors (1-800-288-4677)

ISBN: 978-0-595-43959-1 (pbk)
ISBN: 978-0-595-88279-3 (ebk)

Printed in the United States of America

Dedicated to my parents, family and friends

C ONTENTS

▼

CHAPTER 1

▼

CHOOSING THE RIGHT SHIP AND ITINERARY FOR YOU

With several hundred cruise ships sailing the waters of the world, first time cruisers and even more seasoned cruisers often find selecting the right cruise overwhelming. And, what might have been the right cruise for your co-worker Sally, might not be the right ship or itinerary for you. So, how do you select one for your hard earned vacation?

First begin by checking out the websites of the various cruise lines. And, take your time, really go through it well and read what each cruise line and what each ship within the cruise line has to offer. For example, going on Disney Wonder might be an excellent choice for a family with children under 10 but, if it's just the adults going … you might be put off by the lack of an onboard casino and feeling over-run by families with small children. So, it's extremely important to do research based on your needs.

Here is a list of cruise lines that appeal to the widest audiences. These are the official cruise line websites:

Cruise Lines	Website
Carnival Cruise Line	www.carnival.com
Celebrity Cruise Line	www.celebrity.com
Costa Cruise Line	www.costacruises.com
Crystal Cruise Line	www.crystalcruises.com
Cunard Cruise Line	www.cunard.com
Disney Cruise Line	www.disney.com/disneycruise/index.html
Holland America Line	www.hollandamerica.com
Norwegian Cruise Line	www.ncl.com
Oceania Cruise Line	www.oceaniacruises.com
Princess Cruise Line	www.princess.com
Royal Caribbean Cruise Line	www.royalcaribbean.com
Seabourn Cruise Line	www.seabourn.com
Windjammer Cruises	www.windjammer.com
Windstar Cruise	www.windstarcruises.com

As you go through the various websites and begin realizing just how different each cruise line is … the next thing you'll need to decide is what you really want out of your cruise vacation. Are you looking to just really unwind and, not do much of anything except relax and be pampered? If this is the case, I'd suggest looking for an itinerary with more days at sea than in port. On the other hand, if you're afraid you'll be bored and want to visit new places and see new things then, I would suggest looking for a more port intensive cruise (meaning a cruise that offers lots of stops).

In general, I would suggest trying one of the mainstream cruise lines for the first time cruiser. This means Carnival Cruise Lines, Celebrity Cruise Lines, Disney Cruise Lines, Holland America Cruise Line, Norwegian Cruise Lines, Princess Cruise Lines or Royal Caribbean Cruise Lines. While each line has it's own unique features and personality, all of them offer:

- Larger and Newer Vessels

- A variety of staterooms (also known as cabins) with something for nearly every budget

- Various activities ranging from belly flop contests to art auctions

- Evening shows in the main theater

- Casino (on most ships, Disney and a few NCL ships being the exceptions to the rule)

- Various dining choices

- Childrens and Teen Programs

- A disco

- Friendly, helpful crew and officers (just don't expect them to bend over backwards for you)

In the end, regardless of which cruise line and ship you select, there is an extremely high chance you're going to love it and return to another cruise vacation. If you're still confused and still need direction then I suggest checking out the <u>CLIA (Cruise Line International Association)</u> website. Here you will find the answers to most of your questions regarding cruising, and, you can also catch up on all the latest cruise news!

CHAPTER 2

▼

BOOKING A CRUISE: YOUR OPTIONS

Travel Agent vs. Booking Direct With The Cruise Line

You finally decided you're ready to book a cruise. Do you book with the cruise line directly or do you book through a travel agency? Which is better? It's a personal choice and it depends on how much control you like in booking your trip.

The advantage of booking directly with the cruise line is that you can pick out the ship, dates, and cabin with no one trying to persuade you to try something else. Additionally, some people feel more secure when dealing with the cruise line directly—this part is a misconception—travel agents are just as trust worthy with your personal information as the cruise line, and, it's an unfounded fear that all travel agents are going to run off with your personal information and credit card number and go on a spending spree. If the travel agency has a CLIA number, they have been bonded. So, unless you are complete control freak, there are very few advantages to booking directly with the cruise line.

The advantages of booking with a travel agent can be many—the trick is finding a good agent. A good agent will work for you—from getting the cruise line to reduce your rate if a price drop occurs to helping you out if you find yourself missing your plane to the ship to sending you a token "thank you" gift in your cabin. You might find a good agent on your first try or you might try 20 different agents before you find the right one for you.

One of the biggest mysteries seems to be that people aren't exactly sure how travel agents get paid. Agents are paid commission on everything they sell, well nearly everything. If you are booking a cruise, it is the cruise line—not you who pays the travel agent.

> Side Note: *In general, travel agencies (and it is VERY important to note that it is the agency, not that agent) are paid 10% of the sale, so, if your cruise cost is $1000 for a four night cruise, the travel agency is earning $100, and, out of that the booking agent earns a percentage as set by the agency owner.* So, if you believe travel agents are making a fortune, think again … they love what they do but, they aren't going to get rich doing it.

I hope I've taken some of the mystery away about how travel agents make their money and, I hope I have given you enough information to decide if you're a hands type who'd rather book directly with the cruise line or if you'd rather the professional assistance of a travel agent. Either way, one thing is for certain, more than likely you're going to get hooked on cruising! It truly does become an addiction …

CHAPTER 3

▼

INTERNET TRAVEL AGENCIES: HOW TO KNOW THEY ARE THE REAL DEAL

All to often people question whether or not an internet travel agency is "real". Almost always the answer is "yes"! I don't know why but, some people have a very hard time believing that an internet based travel agency is legitimate so I am going to attempt to clear up the mysteries of how it all works. Most internet travel agencies are REAL travel agents who are working out of their homes. These travel agents work with a Host Company. The host company carries all the business licenses and registrations which cover all agents. The agents are usually referred to as independent contractors and, the agent usually uses a different company name than the host company to identify their bookings within the host company.

So, now that you know a little bit about how it works for the agent, here is how to tell if the company is legitimate:

1. It might seem oblivious but, ask the travel agent if they are working with a host agency. If the answer is yes, then you need to ask the travel agent for their Registered Seller of Travel numbers, less than a handful of states require these, however, they are an important part of establishing the legitimacy of a travel agency. Most internet agencies will have at least one of these numbers and will look something like this: CST # 1234567-89

2. You also want to verify the host company information, so, you can ask the agent for their <u>CLIA (Cruise Line International Association)</u> number. Some agents may not give this out, and, that's ok, you can STILL check by visiting: <u>http://www.cruising.org</u> and plugging in the zip code for the host agency (this will be found in the lower right hand corner in the blue box). If the agent refuses to provide either the zip code or the actual CLIA number, then you might have a problem and, you may want to seek out another travel agency. Why? Simply put CLIA is one of the regulating boards that oversees the travel industry, specifically dedicated to cruising. There are other governing agencies such as <u>IATA</u>, however, if you are booking a cruise, it is the CLIA information you want to verify.

3. Once you verify the host company, **you can rest assured you are dealing with a legitimate travel agency**. CLIA has very high standards and they just don't let anyone off the street register as a cruise agency. Now is the time to ask your internet agent if they charge any fees. *If they do, then you'll want to get that information in writing and, expect to see charges listed on your credit card statement from the host agency.* Some legitimate charges an agent can make are: shipping and handling fees, late booking fees, arranging air transportation or hotels, group fees, name change fees, and cancellation fees. If your agent does not charge for these services, then the only charges you should see on your credit card statement should be DIRECTLY FROM THE CRUISE LINE. PERIOD. *If your agent tells you that they do not charge fees and then all of a sudden you see fees from the agency and, you have it in writing that no service fees are charged, cancel your booking immediately and change travel agents. You'll save yourself a huge headache later on!*

By doing these few simple steps you can be guaranteed that you are dealing with a registered, real life travel agency. While I do understand the hesitation of booking with an unknown person or agency, you as the consumer must also realize that it takes time and effort on the agent's part to give out this information and put to the consumer's mind at ease. If you continue to have doubts, do both yourself and internet agent a favor, go to another agency, maybe one in your hometown. Chances are you won't get the lower prices that the internet agency can offer because the traditional travel agency has lots of overhead including: rent, electric, renter's insurance, city or town business fees, and the list goes on and on. And, if you think the "big" nationwide agencies are going to offer better prices and service, think again, very often they have the most complaints and more than likely you won't get the service you expect once they've made the sale. Large travel agencies are only concerned with the bottom line: sales and revenue. Once they have you booked, they aren't going to worry about you, they are going to worry about their next sale. It's a sad statement for a service industry but it's true. This is one case where bigger isn't necessarily better.

CHAPTER 4

▼

BOOKING YOUR CRUISE

If you are booking your cruise vacation online, most cruise lines and travel agencies that offer online reservations make the process very easy, giving step by step instructions along the way. If you have decided to book with a travel agent, he or she will ask you for some necessary information such as legal names, dates of birth, if you'd like air transportation to your embarkation point, if you'd like to purchase insurance (highly recommended), your payment information and your travel agent will be able to answer any questions you might have at that time.

Unless you are booking after what is known as Final Payment*, then you will only need to place a deposit. While deposits range greatly, in general, cruises that are 5 days in length or under typically have a deposit requirement of $100 per person; cruises that are 7 days in length or longer usually require a $250 per person deposit; and cruises over 7 days in length have deposit requirements of $450 per person. Also, some cruise lines, such as Carnival Cruise Lines, require that you pay for your insurance (which is not mandatory) at the time of deposit as well. If you are booking after the set Final Payment date, then you will need to pay in full.

> *Final Payment is the amount due on the balance of your cruise. Unlike most vacations, your cruise is paid before you leave. Typically, final payments range between 60 to 90 days prior to the departure date of the cruise.

Once you are booked, you will receive a confirmation number. Your confirmation number not only gives you a tracking record of your credit card payment, it also allows access to check out your reservation online (this applies to most major cruise lines); and, you'll be able to book shore tours (if your selected cruise line allows this option); plus, you can pre-register your information such as your passport number (most cruise lines are now requiring this step, check with your specific cruise line for details). And, now you can start looking forward to your cruise.

It's that simple. It's that easy!

CHAPTER 5

▼

AIR TRANSPORTATION OPTIONS AND AIRPORT/PIER TRANSFERS

Most people usually have to fly to the city where their cruise begins. There are two options if you need to fly. You can purchase air through the cruise line or you can book your air on your own. Which is better? It's a tough call and it's a very personal choice.

I usually book my own air because almost always I fly into the city where my cruise is beginning at least one day prior to the actual sailing date. Why? Well, I like to have that safety net of time being on my side, and, this way if there are any unforeseen delays such as mechanical problems with the plane or weather related problems like snow or heavy fog where flights can be delayed for hours, if not completely canceled, then I literally still have time to spare. However, you can still take advantage of flying in early through the cruise line … if they are offering a pre-cruise package … that option isn't always available. It's usually cheaper for me to book my own air and, I have more control over the routing, I prefer non-stops and, I am willing to pay for it. The money I spend for one night in a hotel is well worth the piece of mind I receive by handling my air transportation in this way.

The main advantage for booking your air through the cruise line is that the cruise line will hold the ship, for a reasonable amount of time, should your flight be delayed. The other advantage is that your airport/pier transfers are included with this service, thus, eliminating the worry of how you're going to get to the pier once you're in the city where the cruise will begin. The down side? Usually you'll pay more, sometimes much more, than the airfares you can find on your own and, more than likely you're going to get the worst possible route and more than likely will be required to change planes.

Side Note: Airport/Pier transfers can usually be purchased even if you book your own air. Check with your cruise line for full details and prices.

CHAPTER 6

▼

PACKING FOR YOUR CRUISE

Travel Documents and other items to keep with you

- airline tickets or e-ticket confirmation

- cruise documents (if e-documents are issued be sure to print out a copy to take with you)

- passports and visas (if necessary) or proof of citizenship (check with your cruise line for requirements)

- vaccination certificate (if required)

- driver's license and auto insurance card—in case you decide to rent a car when ashore

- medical insurance cards and medical history (especially if traveling alone)

- copy of prescriptions and list of all medicines you are taking

- another picture ID—if you don't take driver's license

- credit cards—be sure to call credit card companies before traveling to alert them you are traveling outside your normal area

- ATM card

- pre-paid phone card

- cash or traveler's checks

- 3 copies of airline tickets, cruise tickets, passports/visas, itinerary—pack 1 copy in carry on, 1 copy in checked luggage, and leave one copy with someone at home

- contact numbers to report lost/stolen credit cards or traveler's checks

- emergency numbers at home

- wallet and/or fanny pack

- watch

Reading Material and Necessities

- glasses and/or contact lenses

- sunglasses

- guidebooks, maps, and other port of call information

- foreign language phrase book or dictionary

- books and/or magazine for leisure reading

- home and email addresses of friends and relatives—for sending postcards, emails, or gifts

Electronics and Cameras

- plug adaptor and converter

- cell phone and charger (cell phones may not work on ships or certain ports of call, check with both your provider and cruise line for full details)

- laptop computer

- binoculars (especially if cruising to places such as Alaska where wildlife and other points of interest can be seen from the ship)

- film and/or digital camera (disposable cameras can be a wonderful alternative on vacations)

- extra memory cards for digital camera

- batteries for digital camera

- battery charger

- I-pod or walkman and CDs (for walking on deck or on treadmill)

- small travel alarm clock—battery operated (chances are there won't be a clock in your cabin)

- night light

Medicine Kit

- prescription drugs and any other essential medications in carry on bag

- ear plugs or "ear planes"

- small first aid kit (band aids, Q-tips, vaseline, dramamine, antibiotic cream, bandages, anti-diarrheal medication, cortisone

- cream, aspirin/tylenol/advil)

- germicidal hand cleaner

- hand lotion

- bug spray (not for your cabin on the ship, but for mosquitoes and other insects you may encounter on shore tours)

- sun screen/sun block and lip sunblock

Other Miscellaneous Items

- duct tape (hundreds of uses—yes really!)

- garbage/laundry bags (for dirty laundry)

- umbrella

- playing cards or other small, portable game (to keep you busy during times such as the debarking process at the end of the cruise)

- shoe horn

- sewing kit for emergency repairs (pack in checked luggage)

- hats/caps/visors

Women's Clothing Packing List

- bras (include strapless if needed for evening wear)

- panties

- lingerie/night gown/pajamas/robe

- socks

- trouser socks or pantyhose or stockings and garter belt

- camisole/slip

- purses (day and evening)

- belts

- scarves

- gloves and hat (if expect cold weather)

- walking shoes or sneakers

- sandals

- dress and/or evening shoes

- costume jewelry

- swim suit

- swim suit cover-up

- thongs/flip flop shoes

- work out clothes

- dress/outfit for informal nights on ship (check with your cruise line for number of nights and definition)

- dress/outfit for formal nights on ship (check with your cruise line for number of nights and definition)

- dress/outfit for casual nights on ship (check with your cruise line for number of nights and definition)

- shorts

- tops of all types (sleeveless, short-sleeved, long-sleeved)

- pants/slacks

- jacket, raincoat, winter coat (depending on time of year and destination)

Women's Miscellaneous Items

- blow dryer (most ships have hair dryers in the cabin but, you might prefer your own)

- curling iron or curlers

- comb/brush

- hair gel or spray

- shampoo (samples are usually provided in your bathroom kit in your cabin)

- conditioner

- shower cap

- deodorant

- toothbrush

- toothpaste

- dental floss

- mouthwash

- tweezers

- make-up mirror

- make-up and make-up bag

- make-up remover

- cleanser

- moisturizer and freshener

- nail polish and remover

- nail clippers and file (be sure to pack in checked luggage)

- razor and shaving cream

- perfume/cologne

Men's Clothing Packing List

- underwear

- pajamas/sleepwear

- socks and don't forget dress socks!

- belts

- gloves and hat (if expect cold weather)

- walking shoes or sneakers

- sandals

- evening or dress shoes

- tuxedo jacket and pants (or dark suit)—check with your cruise line for formal night description

- tuxedo tie, suspenders, and cummerbund

- tuxedo cufflinks/studs

- sport jacket

- regular ties

- tuxedo shirt

- dress shirts

- swim suit/trunks

- work out clothes

- shorts

- casual shirts

- slacks/pants/trousers

- jacket, raincoat, winter coat (depending on time of year and destination)

Men's Miscellaneous Items

- comb/brush

- shampoo (samples are usually provided in your bathroom kit in your cabin)

- deodorant

- toothbrush

- toothpaste

- dental floss

- mouthwash

- tweezers

- nail clippers (be sure to pack in checked luggage)

- razor and shaving cream (or electric razor)

- cologne/after shave

CHAPTER 7

▼

E-DOCUMENTS
FOR
A CRUISE

Like them or not, E-documents are the wave of the future in cruising. So what are E-Documents and how do they work? E-Documents have the same information that a paper ticket has except it is delivered to you through an email or via a link to the cruise line's website where you will be asked to enter specific information to retrieve your reservation and documents. Once you have received the link or email and open it you can print the information and take it to the check in with your proof of identification and citizenship. What's the advantage of E-documents? Should they ever be lost or misplaced, they are easily and quickly replaceable. The down-side? Many people feel like they want to have some more tangible in their hands, like a piece of paper printed from their computer isn't going to be enough. The truth of the matter is—once you get accustomed to the idea, most people do like them … and over the next several years, paper tickets will be phased out altogether.

With E-documents, your name and reservation number are in the cruise line reservation system, just like they are when you receive paper documents. So, all that is happening is eliminating the need to drag a large, bulky package along to the cruise terminal with you. You will still have to provide identification at check-in and, it's just as fast, if not faster than paper tickets when checking in.

I hope this has taken the mystery out of E-documents.

Chapter 8

▼

Checking-In
For Your Cruise

I have a degree in Business and Marketing and, I know one of the first rules of marketing and advertising is selling the strong point and, either lessening or ignoring the bad points. Given that there are so many new cruisers out there (only 15% of the American population has ever taken a cruise and that number drops significantly for the rest of the world), I thought it would be important to fill you in what the checking-in process entails since it's a bit different than checking into a hotel.

Most people want to start their vacations as early as possible and, while most ships begin boarding at noon or 1pm, eager passengers often arrive at the cruise terminal as early as 10 or 10:30 am. Believe me when I tell you, they aren't going to open the ship up any sooner just because their are lots of people waiting to board. What you need to realize is that the ship's crew has only about 4 hours in total to have the old guests leave and the new guests come aboard. During this time, they have to restock, clean, and literally get the ship in ship-shape for the next group of passengers boarding. Not an easy task!

Even if they do start checking you in a bit earlier, there is a good chance you still won't be allowed on the ship but, rather you'll be escorted to a little waiting area where they MIGHT have refreshments … don't count on it unless your a frequent guest of the cruise line or traveling in one of the suites. Personally, I find that if I arrive around 2pm, the lines to check-in are much shorter and, I am not herded into the holding pen area, I can immediately board the ship.

So, let's go over the check-in process, I know I was unnerved my first cruise because I didn't know what to expect so I hope I can take that anxiety away for some of you out there you might have the same first cruise jitters. Step one is getting to the pier itself. Keep in mind that even if you make your own flight arrangements you can still purchase transfers from airport to the pier through the cruise line. Prices vary so check with your travel agent or cruise line.

Cruise line transfers are usually the easiest but, not necessarily the cheapest way to get to the pier. There will be cruise lines representatives in uniform with cruise line signs in the airport, these people are usually located in the luggage carousel area. You simply approach the cruise line representative, tell him or her which ship you are on, and, they will tell you were to go after you've picked up your luggage from your flight. You'll then proceed to the bus where you hand over your luggage to the staff, if you haven't done so already, now is the time to get those luggage tags for the cruise on your bags!

Now, don't panic, this will be the last time you see your luggage until AFTER you've boarded the ship. (That is why it is so important to make sure your luggage tags are filled out COMPLETELY, CORRECTLY, and PLACED ON YOUR LUGGAGE). If you have a carry-on (which I recommend everyone should do), you simply do not hand it over and you take it on the inside of the bus with you. Keep in mind, your carry-on is going to have to fit through an x-ray machine similar to those at the airports, so, it can't be too large. And off to the pier you go …

If you're arriving to the pier by private car, limousine or some other method that does not involve cruise line transfers, again, make sure your luggage tags are filled out COMPLETELY, CORRECTLY, and PLACED ON YOUR LUGGAGE before you arrive (if at all possible).

Side Note: there are cases such as in late bookings where your documents must be picked up at the pier or in the case of the new E-Documents where you'll have to put your luggage tags on once you arrive at the pier.

Now you're going to hand over your luggage to one of the porters and, it's customary to tip them $1—$2 PER BAG. Don't gripe about it, just do it. Also, if you have a carry-on, remember to hang on to it and not hand to the porter, again, remember the carry on must be able to fit through the x-ray machine. Which is actually your next step.

Just like at the airport you're going to go through a security line. It's the exact same set up. You'll walk through the metal detector and your bags will go on a conveyor belt through an x-ray machine. Once you're through the security line, you'll be directed to stand in another (hopefully short) line to actually check in.

Now it's your turn to go up to the next available agent. You will need to hand over your passport (forget the days of the driver's license and birth certificate for ID purposes, they are just about gone, beginning in late <u>December, 2006 all cruise passengers will be required to have passports</u>). In addition to your passport, you'll need your reservation number which will be located in your cruise documents (don't worry the agent will know exactly where to find it), and if you're paying for your on board expenses by credit or debit card you will need to present that as well. If you are going to pay your onboard expenses by cash, you can establish your account with the purser's office (also known as they Guest Relations Desk) once you're onboard the ship.

At this time, the agent will retrieve your key. This is going to have the same shape and size as a credit card. It's an extremely vital item so do your best not to lose it!! This little card is going to act as your ID while on the ship, it is going to act as your charge card on the ship, AND, it is your room key. Now do you understand why I said it's a vital item!?

Once that is done, you're going to proceed to another security area. Here you are going to hand over your newly acquired card to the security officer and he or she is going to ask you to look into a box or a camera and before you know what's happening, they are going to snap an awful picture of you! And, you'll hear a delightful "bing-bong" as this is being done. Get accustomed to doing this....

every time you leave the ship and every time you re-enter the ship, you are going to be required to do this … even the crew has to do it. It's for your own safety and, it also helps the ship to know if anyone is late or missing when the ship is ready to set sail for the next port of call. Personally, I LOVE hearing that "bing bong"—that's the first sign your vacation has started!

Ok, I promise, you're almost done and ALMOST ready to step aboard your cruise ship. Now comes the part I absolutely hate with a passion. Your Welcome Aboard photo. Let's face it, you've been traveling all day, standing in line after line…. you're going to look … well, not good … and at the worst possible minute, that's when they'll snap your photo. Grin and bear it. You are under no obligation to purchase this or any photos they might take of you while onboard.

Finally! You're onboard! Depending on the cruise line, you might be escorted to your cabin or you might be left on your own to find your cabin. If you are left on your own and get lost, just ask! The crew knows the ship is large and often confusing and they'll gladly point you in the right direction, if not take you there themselves. And, don't worry, it might take a while but, your luggage will eventually show up. Just don't expect it immediately! Don't even expect it in time for dinner, especially if you have first seating!

So that about sums up the check-in process. It's not hard, just long and tedious … and I hope I've taken some of the mystery out of the entire process.

CHAPTER 9

▼

YOUR CABIN

Side Note: Depending upon what time your board the ship, your cabin may or may not be ready when you board. If it isn't ready, other public areas such as the buffet will be open and an announcement will be made when your cabin is ready.

After finding your way through a maze of long corridors, you'll finally find your cabin. First time cruisers, be prepared—chances are it is going to be smaller than you expected. However, this is not the time to get upset or panic. The truth of the matter is that a lot of time and effort has gone into the design of your cabin and, you're going to be shocked how much storage room really is available. And, the reality is that most passengers are only in their cabins to sleep, change and shower.

Usually within a few minutes of you arriving at your cabin, you'll have a knock at the door. More than likely this is your cabin attendant coming to introduce him or her self. Simply put, your cabin attendant is your housekeeper. If you experience any problems such as a dipping sink or need extra pillows or towels, this is the person to contact. Overall, your cabin attendant is rarely seen and, yet, somehow manages to keep everything impeccable!

CHAPTER 10

▼

YOUR BATHROOM

A little bit back, I explained that when advertising a service or a product the idea is focus on the positive and hide or lessen the negative. While this isn't exactly a negative aspect of cruising, it most certainly is a bit of a shock for the first time cruiser. I am referring to the bathroom found in your cabin. Small doesn't even begin to describe these little wonders …

I call them little wonders because it is amazing what the design engineers are able to fit into such a small space. With the exception of bathrooms found in suites, your private bathroom in your cabin is going to be a tight fit for one person, so, forget trying to "share" the bathroom at the same time.

In almost every private cabin bathroom on a cruise ship, you will find a toilet, sink, of course towels, perhaps a small basket of samples such as shampoo or aspirin, and then, stuffed in the corner you will find an unbelievably small shower stall usually with a curtain but sometimes with a door.

Ladies, you're going to find it a challenge to shave your legs in this tight compartment, it's dark so you might be prone to "miss" a spot and, you're going to learn how to contort your legs and body in unique positions just to get the job done! Gentlemen, especially you taller fellows, are going to find showering a challenge too … all too often you will have to bend or squat down to rise off, especially if you're washing your hair. If you're lucky, your shower will feature a detachable hand-held shower head sprayer to help make things easier.

While the toilet appears innocent enough, it too has it's own unique features. Most noticeably the "flusher" is usually a big button, usually located in back when the lid is in the down position. And, the flushing action is that of suction to the point where you think the entire cabin might be flushed down with it!

Another word of warning, unless your in a physically disabled cabin, you are going to have to step up to your bathroom. For most people this appears to be no big deal at first but, it will become a big deal in the middle of the night when you're still half asleep and nature calls. So, you'll stumble out of bed and shuffle along to the bathroom and all of a sudden WHACK! You've stubbed your toe! So, just try to put it in the back of your head and, maybe you'll avoid this misfortune.

The funniest part about your cabin bathroom is the effect it is going to have on you when you return home. No longer will you complain that your bathroom is too small. All of a sudden it is going to appear huge to you! Additionally, for the first night or two you are back home, you are going to instinctively try to "step up" when entering and "step down" when leaving. Don't worry, it does pass quickly when your brain finally accepts the fact that your vacation is over …

CHAPTER 11

▼

THE SUITE LIFE

One of the more frequently asked questions about cruising is regarding the suites on-board cruise ships. People often are curious about what the appeal and the perks are if a suite is booked. The answer is—it varies from cruise line to cruise line. In almost all cases, suites are larger, sometimes much larger than inside, outside, and even balcony cabins. Additionally, most of the time they feature a full bathroom that includes a shower/tub combination and sometimes even a separate shower and whirlpool tub. This is opposed to the small shower that is in other categories.

In addition to the extra square footage of the cabin, many times booking a suite means receiving "perks". These perks can range from a butler (yes, really, a butler) to a private lounge where only suite passengers may be admitted. It also often means priority: boarding privileges, luggage delivery, and tendering.

Side Note: *Tendering is when the lifeboats are used to transport passengers from ship to shore—this is only done when the ship is too large or there aren't enough berths in the port for your ship to dock.*

Is it worth it? That's a highly personal decision but, for many people the answer is yes. In fact, in most cases, suites are usually the first categories to sell out on any given cruise, of course, there are exceptions but, as a thumb rule, if you want a suite—book early … and very early for peak cruising times such as Christmas, New Year's or Easter week … meaning at least one year or more in advance.

So who books suites? Honeymooners; those celebrating a special occasion such as retirement, a birthday or wedding anniversary; those who like the finer things in life and expect no less on vacation; and those who want to be very pampered while on vacation.

The main drawback about booking a suite? It's hard to go back to anything "less"! So, if you have the means, go ahead—and, enjoy the suite life!

CHAPTER 12

▼

THE LIFEBOAT DRILL AND OTHER THINGS TO DO BEFORE THE SHIP SETS SAIL

For some reason a lot of people have the misconception that cruising is very regimented: eat now, go here now, go to bed ... well, surprise, surprise ... it's nothing like that all! Well, except maybe if you're in the Navy but, then again that's no pleasure cruise! On a cruise ship, it's really all about you and what you want out of your vacation. However, there is one thing that you absolutely must do: Attend the lifeboat drill. Maritime law requires that this be held within 24 hours of departure but, so far, every single cruise I've ever taken has had the lifeboat drill before the ship ever left the pier on embarkation day. Yes, you MUST attend. Why? For your own safety, and, if you think you can sneak up to your cabin and hide there until it's over ... think again. Cabin attendants check all the staterooms as the call to assemble comes over the loudspeaker, and, most cruise lines cross reference you by checking your cabin number off as you form lines for the lifeboat drill. (Your cabin number is printed right on your life-jacket).

More than likely your life-jackets will be waiting for you in plain sight when you first come into your cabin on embarkation day. You can't miss them, they are the big, ugly orange things. If they aren't in plain sight, chances are they are in one of your closets, if you still can't find them, ask your cabin attendant for assistance. You can find where to report on the back of your cabin door. The place you report is called your Muster Station. But, don't get all tense about this, the call to assemble for the drill won't come until about an hour before it's time to set sail, and crew members will be all over the ship directing you where to go.

Now I hope I didn't intimidate or scare anyone off from cruising. The lifeboat drill is more of an annoyance than anything else. It only lasts about 15 minutes and, all you have to do is stand there with your life-jacket on and listen to the crew members as they instruct you on what to do in case of a true emergency.

Side Note: if you or anyone traveling with you is noise sensitive, just be prepared because the Captain is going to blow the ship's horn several times during the life-boat drill and it's loud!

So now that's you visited your cabin, found your life-jackets and sigh … wonder how long it will be until your luggage arrives, you have a variety of things you may want to do. For most people, after checking out there cabin, the next stop is the buffet (if you haven't done so already).

The buffet on embarkation day is often mass chaos since you'll be traveling with both old pro's and first timers. The hardest part is usually trying to locate a seat. I've found the best strategy is to locate a table first, and, then hit the buffet in shifts, this way someone always has claim to the table and can watch everyone's belongings such as cameras and purses. If there are truly no empty tables to be found, ask if you may join people already at a table, almost always they'll say yes and, it's a great way to meet your fellow passengers!

Other things you might want to do before the ship gets under way are make any reservations you need throughout the cruise. Some of the activities that will require reservations are: Dinner at the Specialty Restaurant (or restaurants, many of today's newer ship's offer more than one specialty restaurant … I highly recommend doing this early, especially if cruising during a high demand time such as Christmas or New Year's. The specialty restaurants fill up fast because many people want to mark the day with an extra special dining experience). The beauty salon is also another high priority, especially if you plan on having a special hair-do for Formal Night, these days are in high demand, especially between 3pm and 6pm, so book early! The spa is also a location that requires reservations and days at sea fill up first and they fill up fast.

Once you have all your reservations in place and have visited your cabin and buffet, now is an excellent time to start exploring the ship and, I do recommend taking your camera with you. Often times the public areas will be quiet with no one in them, making it an excellent time to snap some photos of the interior of the ship. You might want go up to the top decks and check out the pool area, perhaps gets some photos of your embarkation port from the ship.

Then before you know it, the Cruise Director will come over the loudspeaker and announce that it's time for the lifeboat drill, and, soon after that you'll be under way. There is nothing as freeing as watching the ship pulling away from the dock … at that point, your vacation has begun. This your time, enjoy yourself!

CHAPTER 13

▼

MEET YOUR CRUISE DIRECTOR

Many of us had our first taste of cruising through the television series "The Love Boat". Well you can pretty much forget everything you saw on "The Love Boat". The crew on most cruise ships are usually forbidden to socialize in a non-professional way with the passengers, of course, there are exceptions but, they are few and far between. And, your cruise director more than likely isn't going to be a pretty, perky "she" … nope, in reality, you'll have a wise-cracking "he" cruise director.

While the Cruise Director somehow manages to make the job look fun and easy, the truth is, he (or she) has one of the most demanding jobs on the ship. So, first time cruisers, are sometimes disappointed when the Cruise Director doesn't get to know them on a more—Julie McCoy—personal type of way.

So what is it that a Cruise Director does? The Cruise Director helps set the overall mood of the ship. He or she works with the entertainers, the Captain, and basically every department on the ship from housekeeping to the restaurant and bar staff. The best Cruise Directors are multi talented and can multi-task from being a public relations specialists to being an Entertainer all within an 18 hour work day! And most of all—cruise directors work very hard to make sure the passengers are having fun!

Some people don't believe a Cruise Director makes that much difference … I disagree, in general, I've found the better the Cruise Director has been, the better the cruise was overall. Unfortunately, like most of the crew on cruise ships, the Cruise Director is regularly rotated throughout the fleet. So, even if you have a wonderful Cruise Director on a specific ship, there is no guarantee that he or she will be there the next time you return to that ship.

Overall, Cruise Directors are hammy, and, I mean that in only the most respectful way. It's take a person who is a bit of a ham to be a good cruise director, you not only have to be able to communicate and convey information well … you also need to be a bit of an actor and those who have the comedic touch truly make wonderful Cruise Directors. And, I applaud you all!

CHAPTER 14

▼

FOOD, GLORIOUS FOOD

One of the misconceptions about cruising is that it's all about food ... and to a point it's true, so, let's review what all the fuss is regarding food and cruising.

Many first time cruisers are stunned to find out that their food (with a few minor exceptions) is included with the price of your cruise fare. That's right, breakfast, lunch, dinner, snacks, even room service is INCLUDED with your cruise price.

Most cruise lines offer a wide variety of food from morning until night. You'll have a choice of a buffet or dining room service for breakfast and lunch, and, dinner varies from cruise line to cruise line. Some cruise lines offer an optional buffet for dinner and others offer table service in the buffet area that isn't as formal as the main dining room, and, of course, the main dining room is always open for dinner.

Which is better? Buffet or the Main Dining Room? It's a very personal choice. For me, I prefer the more formal settings of the main dining and, unless I have shore tours, I will select the main dining room for breakfast, lunch and dinner. I, personally, like the extra service of being waited upon, but, I do agree that there are times when the buffet is more fitting and appropriate for my needs of the day.

Side Note: most cruise lines have an "open" table policy for breakfast and lunch in the main dining room. What this means is that they will sit you at the first available table, often with people you don't know. Some people are uncomfortable with this situation since it is a "forced" socialization. I am not a morning person, so, I always ask if I can have a private table when I enter. Sometimes they'll comply and other times they apologize and still put you at a large table of strangers. I don't mind if I have to eat with others for breakfast and lunch but, given the choice, I do prefer my own company or the company of those I am traveling with ... at least for breakfast.

Dinner time comes with an assigned table and an assigned time. When you make your cruise reservations most lines will ask your dining preferences: early, which is usually around 6pm, or late, which is usually around 8pm.

Side Note: some Carnival and Holland America ships actually offer 4 seatings at dinner, which are first early around 6:00pm, then a second early which is around 6:30pm, and followed by first late seating around 8:00pm and second late seating around 8:30pm.

Also when you first make your cruise reservations, you might be asked if you want a large or a small table. I've been at both and, it's my personal preference to dine with those whom are traveling with me, so I always ask for a small table. Depending on the cruise line and even more specifically the ship, you can request a table for two but, these are few and far between. If you truly wish to snag a table for two, see the Maitre D as soon as you board the ship!

It's good to check your Room Key Card when you first board because most cruise lines imprint your table and dining time right on the front. Be sure to cross reference the table and the dining times assigned to you with those who might be traveling with you. If for any reason there is a mix-up and someone in your traveling party who you wish to dine with is assigned to a different table or time, you need to see the Maitre D as soon as possible to make the necessary changes.

Additionally, if you were assigned second seating and requested first or large table instead of a small one, you should also see the Maitre D as soon as possible after boarding the ship. While the Maitre D will do his or her very best to accommodate your wishes to switch dining times or even tables, this cannot be guaranteed. So that is why if you detect a problem with your dinner request, you'll have a much higher chance of having the problem corrected if you visit the dining room and Maitre D early!

One of the best things about cruising is usually the food service. Now I am not telling you to expect gourmet cooking, it simply isn't going to happen, not on a ship with 2,000–3,000 passengers. However, what you will find is usually a nice selection of appetizers, soups, salads, and entrees. Here's the best part … ORDER AS MUCH AND AS MANY OF EVERYTHING AS YOU LIKE! Ordered something you don't care for after tasting it? Tell your waiter. He or she will gladly obtain something else for you without a blank of an eye. Really liked that prime rib? Tell your waiter! He'll bring a second round for you … usually with a big smile! Have a big appetite? This is no time to be shy! Go ahead! Order two appetizers and two entrees. Eat as much or as little as you like … it's already paid for in your cruise fare!

If you are traveling with a fussy eater or you yourself are a fussy eater, again, not to worry, most cruise ships offer an "always available" section on the menu and these tend to feature standard favorites of the American traveler. The most common items found in the "always available" section are usually steak, pasta, chicken and possibly fish. If you or someone traveling with you has special dietary needs, still no worries. Most cruise ship dining room menus feature items that are heart/fitness healthy (sometimes called the Spa Menu), they also offer vegetarian (but not necessarily vegan) selections, and, if you have other special needs, tell your reservationist or travel agent to note it in your reservation and then visit the Maitre D when you board and, just remind your waiter on the first evening. They will do everything can to provide you with a meal based on your needs.

The are some cruise ships that now offer alternative restaurants, and, almost always these have a charge of around $20—$30 per person. The reason some people are willing to pay this extra charge is that the food quality, the presentation, and the service usually equal that of a 4 or even 5 star restaurant on land. These restaurants do require reservations and, it is wise to make them right after you board the ship, especially if traveling during times such as Christmas, New Year's Eve, Valentine's Day or any other major holiday where people might like to take advantage of these restaurants to help mark the occasion with an extra special meal.

In addition to the main dining room and buffet, most cruise ships also offer pizza, ice cream, and, a grill where you can get hamburgers and hot dogs. The hours these items are offered vary greatly ship to ship so to find out when you can visit these various food venues, simply check your daily newsletter that will be placed in your cabin every night by your cabin attendant. Not only does this newsletter tell you the events of the following day, it will tell you what the requested style of dress is for dinner and, the hours of operation for the dining rooms and other food venues.

Also, most cruise ships offer 24 hour room service. There is no charge for room service and there is no extra charge for the food you might order from room service but, be prepared to be charged if you order drinks, these are rarely complimentary. And just remember, it is customary to tip the person delivering your food to your room $1—$2 in cash. A room service menu will be located in your cabin, usually some place close to the telephone.

So, these are the basics of cruise ship food venues and what to expect. Every ship, even within the same cruise is going to vary slightly, but, overall you will more than likely experience some good dinners and other meals and snacks on your cruise. Enjoy!

CHAPTER 15

▼

ALTERNATIVE RESTAURANTS: ARE THEY WORTH THE EXTRA COST?

There has been a trend over the past several years to offer alternative dining selections onboard cruise ships, the most popular of these alternatives are the specialty restaurants that are only open for dinner. So, what exactly can you expect in specialty restaurants on cruise ships?

Alternative restaurants all have one thing in common … a cover charge. Usually in the $20 to $30 per person range. Additionally, some have restrictions on children's ages (for example <u>Royal Caribbean</u> has a policy that only children 13 years old and older may dine in the specialty restaurant.) Furthermore, reservations are required and usually there is a requested dress code.

Dining in the specialty restaurants on a cruise ship can often match or even surpass dining in a 4 or even 5 star restaurant; and, for those in the know, the $20 or $30 per person charge is almost always worth the extra money. From the outstanding service to the extraordinary quality of the food, it is a fraction of the cost that an equivalent meal would be in a restaurant on land.

This dining experience should not be rushed and often times the cruise lines will recommend allowing 2 to 3 hours to fully enjoy the atmosphere, the food and the service.

Naysayers often complain that they've already spent enough on their cruise and resent the fact the cruise line is trying to nickel and dime them further for the alternative restaurant experience. Additionally, people try to argue to the fact they can get the same quality food in the main dining room. The truth is—in almost all cases—the alternative restaurants ARE a step or two higher in quality than the main dining room … making it well worth the surcharge. Funny thing is—the people who challenge or put down the alternative restaurant concept are the people have never tried them. *To them, I simply say "Don't Knock It Until You've Tried It"!*

While this a very personal choice, I do highly recommend trying the specialty restaurant or restaurants (some ships feature more than one alternative restaurant) and then judge for yourself. Chances are you'll wonder why you didn't try it sooner!

CHAPTER 16

▼

BOREDOM? ON A CRUISE SHIP? NOT LIKELY!

You've probably watched the television commercials for various cruise lines with someone smiling as they are going down a sliding board, or racing past the camera on a jet-ski, or doing something else that looks like the actors are having way too much fun. And, if you're the skeptical type, you're probably thinking that's not what really happens on a cruise ship. And, if you believe this misconception and believe you'll be bored, then this chapter is for you!

I was talking to an acquaintance of mine, someone I would describe as well traveled and, someone who has lived abroad for many, many years. I was just about floored when he sincerely thought that a cruise was just about floating around on the ocean—never realizing how much there is to do on a cruise ship or that you aren't going to be floating around aimlessly for your vacation without ever getting off the ship! Needless to say, I corrected him immediately!

First and foremost, unless you're on a cruise to nowhere (and this is the only time where you'll float about the ocean without a destination and this type of cruise only lasts one or two nights at most), you WILL have destinations (or ports of call) included in your cruise where you may get off the ship (if you chose to do so) and go sightseeing and participate in various activities. And, there is PLENTY to do on a cruise ship!

My acquaintance was further amazed at how many activities are offered on the ship itself. He was under the impression the only things to do are: eat, sunbathing, maybe a swim in the pool and then eating again. Well, I showed him differently! Not with the cruise line brochures, they don't tell you the real story … I gave him this link: http://www.cruisedailies.com/portal/

You just might want to bookmark this link because it gives REAL daily newsletters from various cruise lines which includes all the needed information of the day plus a list of the daily activities! I showed him how to use it … simply go over to the blue box in the upper left hand corner, and click on the folder that says "Cruise Lines", then you select the cruise line which interests you. In this case, we selected Royal Caribbean … from there we were given a list of available newsletters on various ships, so I clicked on Explorer of the Seas and it displayed one newsletter for the June 2, 2006 sailing to the Eastern Caribbean so I clicked "View". Once you're here, locate where it says LINKS on the right hand side and you're going to see Page 1, Page 2, Page 3, and Page 4.

These are all the pages available in the newsletter for viewing for that particular date. So, we clicked on pages 1 and 2 and he wasn't overly impressed, then we clicked on page 3 for June 3, 2006, which happened to be a day at sea. Here on page 3, he saw the hours of operation for the shops, casino, food venues, and more and, I could hear the change of opinion in his voice. Then we click on page 4, and, that's what changed his mind … he could not believe the activities available during a day at sea from early morning until late at night!

So if you're the type that believes that you're going to be bored on a cruise ship, do yourself a favor and at least check out these daily activities newsletters. You might just change your mind … my friend did … I'm sure you just might too!

CHAPTER 17

▼

SHORE EXCURSIONS: INDEPENDENT VS. SHIP SPONSORED TOURS

One of the few things not covered by the price of your cruise ticket are Shore Tours. These are the optional things you can do when you pull into port. There are two types of shore tours—those offered through a cruise line approved company and those you book or do on your own. So what's the difference between the two?

Tours that are offered by the cruise line are NOT actually owned or run by the cruise line but, rather independent companies that the cruise line contracts to provide these services to the passengers. The advantage of booking through the cruise line is that if for any reason your shore tour is running late, the ship will be held for passengers who have been delayed and will not leave port without them. To the first time cruiser this might sound silly but, on every single cruise I've ever taken … in every single port … there is literally at least one passenger who is running for the ship just when it's about to leave. The urgency here is that it is YOUR total responsibility to be back to the ship BEFORE it sails, and, if you miss the ship, it is YOUR responsibility to pick up the cost (not to mention the hassle) of getting to the next port to meet up with the ship. The down size to booking through the cruise line is that the tours are often overpriced and sometimes not well organized.

This brings us to your second option going off on your own or booking a private shore excursion. *SOMETIMES* you'll save money by booking your own shore tour but, if you're the type the runs late or gets easily lost, then you might want to consider booking through the cruise line. While I DO recommend booking through the cruise line, I know many of you are looking for companies that offer shore tours not affiliated with the cruise line. I am going to provide a few but, by no means I am recommending or endorsing any of them. BOOK AT YOUR OWN RISK.

ShoreTours.com

ShoreTrips.com

PortPromotions.com

And, there are many, many companies that offer specific tours (for example deep sea fishing) that are just too vast to even begin to list here. When you do your research be sure to check out the companies reputations before booking.

This brings us to the cost of shore tours. I know most websites avoid giving you the cost and, it is isn't that they are being evasive, it's just that prices change and, what might be correct today, may not be correct tomorrow. Please note the prices I am listing are only examples and, it should be understood by you that prices can and will vary from what I have listed in the example below:

St. Thomas—Island Sightseeing Tour—Length of Time: 2 hours
***Actual sites visited vary with company selected*

ShoreTrips.com $49 per person

PortPromotions.com $28 per person

ShoreTours.com—currently unavailable

Celebrity Cruise Lines—$58 per person

<u>Carnival Cruise Lines</u>—Exact price unavailable

<u>Holland America Cruise Lines</u>—$29 per person

<u>Princess Cruise Lines</u>—$39 per person

Hopefully this brief explanation has given you a bit more insight regarding your shore tour options. The best way to find out about shore tours is to go to the homepage of the specific cruise line you are planning to book or have already booked and, see what is being offered for your specific sailing date.

CHAPTER 18

▼

WHAT HAPPENS WHEN YOUR SHIP OUT OF LUCK

It's been told to you dozens of times throughout your cruise but, you're touch of self-arrogance has you convinced it won't happen to you … Maybe you went off on your own and completely lost track of time … Perhaps you booked a tour with a company other than those hired by the cruise line and you experienced a problem like a flat tire while out on your tour … Or maybe it is a different reason entirely … Whatever the case, you've returned to pier to find your ship has sailed without you. So what happens when you're ship out of luck?

On every cruise, without fail, I've seen no less than half a dozen people literally running for the ship as it's just about ready to leave port. And, often, you'll hear passengers already on board yelling at those who are running "Hurry, Hurry!" … which just adds to the sense of panic those running already feel.

I don't know if I'm just more aware of time than other people but, so far (knock on wood) … I, personally, haven't found myself in this position. However, very unfortunately, occasionally passengers do get left behind because they didn't make it back to the ship on time. So, this is a guide to help you should you ever find yourself in this situation.

After that first gut wrenching moment when you realize you've actually missed the ship, you need to figure out how you're going to catch up with it. This is NOT an easy task! And, it could be indeed very costly. What's that? You say you have insurance? Guess what, you're still ship out of luck! Insurance does NOT cover you if you miss the ship while it's port. **The burden of cost and getting to the next port is solely your responsibility**.

One of the reasons I recommend booking your shore tours through the cruise line is due to this possibility. If for any reason your cruise line sponsored shore tour is late getting back to the ship, they WILL hold the ship for you. If you've gone out on your own or booked through a tour company that isn't affiliated with the cruise line, then it's up to you to get back to the ship on time.

Side Note: A cruise line sponsored shore tour means a tour that you've booked through the cruise line whether you booked through the cruise line website before leaving home or book your tour while on board, they both count as being cruise line sponsored shore tours.

Now, regardless of where you've been stranded, you're going to need to catch up to the ship. Last minute airline tickets are never cheap and they certainly aren't going to be any cheaper for you. Trains or a rental car are SOMETIMES possibilities but, again this isn't going to be inexpensive. The bottom line is … if you're venturing out on your own make sure you have enough money on you (credit cards are best) so you can get to the next port of call if it becomes necessary. But, don't think it's going to be that easy … nope … unless you've taken your passport with you … guess what … not only did you miss the ship but, you're not getting out of the country you're in without a passport. At that point, you'll have to go to your Embassy … which never seems to be open when you need them … to help you expedite a new passport for you. In the meantime, you'll have to find some place to sleep because there is no way your passport is going to be issued to you that same day.

> **Tina's Tip: Even if you don't take your passport with you, at least take a photocopy of your passport with you in case you ever find yourself in this situation, it will help get your new passport to you that much quicker. Also leave a copy of your passport with someone at home who will help you out in such an emergency. Even if you don't find yourself in this type of situation, it is still a very smart idea to leave a copy of your passport with someone at home in case your passport is ever lost or stolen while traveling and, I also recommend keeping a copy of it in your luggage.**

In the meantime, you should call the cruise line and advise them of your situation. The cruise line will then get in touch with the ship so you don't become a listed as missing passenger. This will save everyone (including yourself) headaches later on.

There are going to be cases, such as the cruise is close to coming to an end, that might just be easier to go directly to the port where the ship will end the cruise. You'll still have to go through the same hassles and steps as described above and, all you can do is accept it and, be better prepared the next time …

Now, I hope I haven't scared anyone off from the idea of cruising. The truth is— missing the ship doesn't happen that often. This has merely been a guide to help explain how to proceed should you ever find yourself in this predicament.

And, just remember these few rules while out on tour:

- Always wear a watch that works!

- Make sure you know what time the ship is sailing AND make sure you know the difference between ship's time and local time.

Side note: Often you'll change time zones when on a cruise, ship's time is based on the time zone of the home port of the cruise ship. For example, say your cruise departs from Fort Lauderadale, Florida, you will be on Eastern Time the EN-TIRE cruise, so, when you go to Cozumel, Mexico you will be on Central Time locally but, the ship will sail according to it's Eastern Time Zone clock. In other words, if the cruise director tells you that you'll be sailing at 4:00pm and you're in Cozumel … that means you're actually sailing at 3:00pm local time!

- Take a credit card with you or enough cash to get you to the next port of call if venturing out on your own

- Always take a copy of your passport with you

- If you book a tour with a company other than through those sponsored by the cruise line, ask if they offer some type of guarantee they'll have you back to the ship on time

Follow these simple rules and, you'll be fine!

CHAPTER 19

▼

SHIP BOARD ENTERTAINMENT AND PASSENGER TALENT SHOW NIGHT

I don't why but, for some reason cruise ships thrive on cheesy acts. Perhaps coming from the greater New York area and having seen a number of Broadway productions and having attended many assorted performances at <u>Lincoln Center</u>, I am a bit more jaded in my opinions in this area.

Nonetheless, I have always found the acts on board cruise ships to be—well—cheesy—sorry but it's the only word that fits. Now, don't get me wrong, I have nothing but the utmost respect for the performers—what I want to know is who is in charge of selecting the songs and corn-ball shows that they put on for the passengers? And, why do they have to kill songs with "their" interpretation? I mean, come on, after hearing <u>Van Halen's</u> "Jump" or even <u>Sinatra's</u> "New York, New York" sung by someone who can only be described as a <u>Miss America</u> want-to-be ... It just leaves a bad taste in my mouth and an annoying ringing in my ears. Thanks but, no thanks!

I don't know about you but, I intentionally now miss the shows on purpose, as you can tell it's just not my thing. However, on occasion, I admit, I will stick my head in the door and see what's going on … hoping that maybe "this time" will be something I will enjoy.

There is one time I've never regretted doing this, it was on a Carnival ship on a Bermuda sailing, and, I stepped in the theater to see what was taking place. It turned out to be Passenger Talent Night. I walked in and a woman was giving an outstanding performance of <u>Gloria Gaynor's</u> "I Will Survive". Ok, I was hooked, she was that good, so, I figured I would stay to see the next person … well on walked a young man who I will always remember.

This young man had absolutely no talent. He sang loud and off key, in fact, it wasn't even singing, he half talked the words to his selected song and the rest of the time he was about 2 beats behind the song. What made it worse was the entire audience was laughing at him (you couldn't help it) but, I also couldn't help feel sorry for this young man who honestly seemed to believe he was good. However, now, whenever I hear someone singing that badly, it brings a smile to my face thinking back to that sailing and the show that featured this young man.

And perhaps that's the purpose of these shows … whether it's Passenger Talent Night, A cheesy magician or a production show … that long after you leave, you'll hear a song or see something that reminds you something that took place during a cruise and it puts a smile on your face.

So go ahead! Venture into the show room—you might find something to your liking and maybe not but, that's a beauty of a cruise! There is something for nearly everyone!

As for me, I'll take the delightful DING-DING-DING-DING-DING and the CLANG, CLANG, CLANG that only a slot machine paying out in the casino and maybe catch a show later!

CHAPTER 20

▼

BEWARE OF THE
CHAIR HOGS!

It usually happens on the second day of the cruise. Since the second day of a cruise is almost always a day at sea, you figure you'll sleep in, have a late breakfast, maybe walk around the ship a bit or go to a trivia contest or some other activity and, then you decide you want to go outside and enjoy the sun deck and the pool.

So you proceed back to your cabin, change into your bathing suit, grab your sunscreen and, maybe that book you promised yourself that you'd finish while on vacation, and, head back to the pool. You head outside where the sun hits you directly in the eyes, so, you need a moment to adjust, and, then you begin scanning for a free lounge chair ... You see some with actual people in them but, then you see the rest ... No bodies in the chair but, all types of items to "mark" the chair as taken. You then decide to expand your search and head up one deck, figuring that everyone just wants to be close to the pool.

Once you get up the stairs, you are shocked to see even more "marked" chairs. Now what do you do? The Chair Hogs have taken over!! What is a Chair Hog you ask? A Chair Hog is a very self-centered, often sneaky type of person that is not to be trusted! A good Chair Hog will wake up at a very early hour just to claim a prime chair spot and does so by making the chair look already occupied. The good Chair Hog will stake his claim not by just placing a towel on a chair but, all types of items—books and magazines, sunscreen, maybe even a cheap pair of flip flops and, of course, my favorite, some type of children's toy to help guilt you into not claiming the chair for yourself.

Feeling helpless, you often stand there in disbelief and try to figure out what to do. Do you keep walking around, looking for a truly open chair? The truth is there are only three real choices: give up and go do something else (I don't recommend this, you paid a lot of money for your cruise, you deserve to enjoy every part of the ship just as others do); if you're lucky, you can grab a chair or lounge off the stack and try to find an empty spot to claim as your own; or you can simply displace a Chair Hog.

So, how do you know if someone is really using the chair and perhaps just ran to the bathroom for two minutes versus a true Chair Hog? See, this why I told you that Chair Hogs are sneaky and not to be trusted. There is no way to know! Personally, I start by asking anyone next to the chair that I want if it is occupied. If the answer is yes, then I move on. If the answer is no, I politely gather up all the belongings of the Chair Hog, and place them underneath the chair. When the Chair Hog shows up.... Three hours later ... I just politely smile and the Chair Hog knows that for once, I won!!

I prevent myself from turning into a Chair Hog by simply telling the person next to me that I'm running back to my cabin or going to the bathroom and, that if I'm not back in 15 minutes, my chair is up for grabs. I've found nearly everyone will gladly hold your chair for you if you ask nicely and place a time limit on how long you'll be gone.

Chair Hogs aren't found just by the pools. No, I'm sorry to say you're going to find them throughout the ship. After the pool, the theater is the next biggest venue where you will find these people, often not just saving one or two seats but, trying to save whole rows!!! *Do Not Let Them Intimidate You*! You have just as much right, make that more right because you're actually there in body to claim a seat!! Let them move or let the other members of their party find their own seats!

One case of a Chair Hog that is still very fresh in my memory happened several years ago on a Princess ship during a Christmas sailing. We had started the disembarking process and, a lot people where sitting around the main lobby area waiting for their group to be called. Naturally there were more people than places to sit, that's ok, it was to be expected in this case. Everything was going as it normally does during this time when all of sudden I heard an unbelievable fight breaking out …

A Chair Hog refused to move her packages from a chair so that an elderly gentleman with an oxygen tank could sit down!

I could not believe what I was witnessing!! This woman had the nerve to tell the elderly gentleman and his grown son (who had apparently asked very politely if she would mind removing the bags so his Father could sit) that it was "her" chair and that they should have gotten their earlier. Everyone in that lobby area stood there silently in disbelief to what was taking place. After a shouting match broke out, some of the ships officers finally made it on the scene and escorted the Chair Hog and her group of loud (and foul) mouthed followers off the ship with the next group.

The rest of us stood up, cheered and applauded when they left, and, the ship's officers apologized profusely to the elderly gentleman and his family.

So, the moral to this story is—take no pity on chair hogs. They are just school-yard bullies who never grew up and refuse to believe that they could ever do anything wrong. After all the world was built for them and, we're just lucky they allow us to breath the same air that they do.

I say toss the Chair Hogs all overboard and let the rest of us civilized folks enjoy our cruise without them! It would be good riddance!

CHAPTER 21

▼

A WEIGHTY ISSUE: THERE IS ALWAYS SOMEONE BIGGER THAN YOU ON A CRUISE!

I've never been the type that can consume 8000 calories per day and never put on an ounce of weight. Nope, not me. Like most of you, I just look at food and the weight piles on. So, for the past several years, I try to diet to lose a few pounds before I step foot on a cruise ship, knowing that more likely than not, I will over-indulge. And, while I do this for my own piece of mind, I've noticed one thing … No matter if I've been a skinny size 6 or an overweight size 16, one thing is certain … There will ALWAYS be someone larger than you on a cruise ship!

Now, I'm not picking on anyone. Heaven knows, I've gained and lost more weight over the years that would add up to be another person, and, I've certainly been way overweight from time to time in my lifetime. So, this isn't about saying that being overweight is bad nor is it a judgment in any way. This is merely observation of people who I've seen on cruise ships.

Don't let your size stop you from taking a wonderful vacation! I promise you, there WILL be someone larger than you on the ship!

Oh sure, you're going to see lots of skinny, bikini-clad gals ... most of whom are under 35 and, have little to no shape, often looking like walking ironing boards. However, you're also going to see a large portion (pun intended) of people who are your size and larger. You'll see the Mom around 30 years old, chasing after her 3 year old, now wearing a one piece because of a C-section. You'll see the 50ish woman with her friends in skirted bathing suits, trying to hide their once fabulous legs. And, then, guaranteed ... you'll see the ones that don't care what anyone else thinks! I've seen women, who ought to know better, strutting around in two pieces and mini-skirts, with their belly fat right out there on display. I once saw a woman so large that her rear-end needed it's own zip code and, she thought nothing of it to wear a VERY revealing swimsuit ... it's been years since that cruise and that imagine is still burned in my mind. And, I don't mean any of this in a negative tone. On the contrary! I admire these people! I want to be like them! I want to have enough self confidence to say "Hey this is me, like it or lump it". And, they have the right attitude!

Chances are slim to none that you'll EVER see any of the people you cruise with again in your lifetime! So go ahead, put on those shorts and bathing-suit! I know I'm not going to sit there judging you and, chances are most of the other passengers won't either. There are too many other things to see and do on a cruise ship than to worry about what someone I don't even know is wearing (or not)! And, for the few that might be preoccupied with this past-time ... Would you really want to get to know anyone that shallow? Not me!

So, to all of you sitting at home wishing you were a different size, wishing you looked different. I say put those feelings aside and come out and enjoy life! And, I promise you.... There WILL be someone larger than you on your cruise! It's guaranteed!

CHAPTER 22

▼

WHO IS BILL W.?

While you're looking through your daily cruise newsletter that is placed in your cabin every evening, you'll find lots of information. You'll out what the dress code is for dinner, what the featured shows are for the evening and, the list seems to be never ending ... and, on just about every cruise you're going to see "Friends of Bill W." This often leads to wild guesses of who Bill W really is and why he is always having a meeting some place.

Friends of Bill W. is a code name for Alcoholics Anonymous, and, yes there are meetings on nearly every cruise within the mainstream cruise lines. Times and frequency are going to vary, so, just check your daily newsletter.

I am not including this information in a judgmental way, in fact, just the opposite, I am making sure the word is out there that support is closer than you think, even on vacation ...

CHAPTER 23

▼

IT HAPPENS ON EVERY CRUISE: THE COMPLAINERS

Regardless of the cruise line, regardless how hard you try ... somehow they always manage to find you and sit near you and talk very loudly ... I am, of course, talking about The Complainers. You know them, they bargain shop for their cruise and they book the absolute lowest, cheapest category cabin. And, this isn't because that's all they can afford, that's rarely the case, they just want to be able to complain about EVERYTHING! From their small, windowless cabin to the "horrible" food to the "rough" ocean to the weather!

And these people never say what's on their mind quietly amongst themselves, NO, they speak in loud, often obnoxious tones so that everyone can hear what "they" have to say ... They complain if the drinks are too cold, they complain if there is too much ice or not enough ice; they complain the theater seats are terrible (regardless of how many times they move); they complain about dinner times; they complain about food selections; they complain about food quality; they complain about the ports; they complain there wasn't enough time in the ports, then, they complain there was too much time in the ports; they complain about the dress codes (and never comply themselves but, always are the first to point out others that haven't complied); they complain about the crew; and, they complain about the Cruise Director. They just complain about everything!

There is no easy way to deal with complainers. If you move, for some reason, they move with you. If you give them an icy stare, they become combative and insist that their opinion is the correct opinion! And, if you dare express your opinion, chances are they will become even louder and try to humiliate you. The best solution is to walk away and go to a completely different area and, if you see them, go in the opposite direction.

The funny thing is—the complainers never see themselves as they really are ... They'll complain about "hundreds of unruly children" on-board.... and yet their children are the ring leaders ... because they suffer from "Not My Child" syndrome. They'll complain about the tendering process and demand to be first, when in reality, others were ahead of them or have "passes" such as those often given to those in suites or extremely frequent cruisers of the cruise line which entitles them to priority tendering. They'll complain about the ports and how terrible they are ... and bad mouth the locals ... without justification. They're the first to cut in line and are usually the chair hogs of the cruise too ... all without apology. *After all, they paid for their vacation....* apparently the rest of us are cruising for free!

I am not tolerant of complainers because most of the times they have no basis of complaint and, 99% of the time, they themselves lack common sense, and, are usually rude, thoughtless Neanderthals. They live for insulting and putting down others, and, I certainly do not socialize with this type in my every day living ... I am certainly not going to socialize or tolerate them on my vacation!

No, for me, it's much easier to move than to listen to another word. So to the complainers out there, you go right ahead and do your thing but, you aren't going to bully your way. If I have a certain right, then I am going to put it to use ... and you can complain about ME all you want ... you'll still be complaining about me weeks after your trip because I had the nerve to use my tendering pass and got on before you did ... and I won't have given you a second thought. Why? Because I have better things to do ...

CHAPTER 24

▼

BOOKING YOUR NEXT CRUISE WHILE ON-BOARD YOUR CURRENT CRUISE

One of the most frequently asked questions is what is the advantage of booking your next cruise while on your current cruise. There is usually at least one advantage to booking your next cruise while on your current cruise, and, it's usually some type of booking incentive such as on-board credit and/or sometimes a reduced deposit (or sometimes you get lucky and get both).

Have a favorite travel agent that might feel hurt that you didn't book with them? Not to worry! Your on-board booking can easily be transferred to your travel agent and they will still receive full commission as if they made the booking from the start.

So, how do you book on-board for your next cruise? Nearly every cruise ship as a specific person (sometimes there are more than one) on-board every cruise who will be available specifically to answers your questions and help you book your next cruise while on-board the ship. This information is usually found in your daily newsletter that is left in your cabin. If the information isn't available there—go to the Purser's Desk (sometimes known as the Guest Relations Desk) and ask to be directed to the right person.

Often there are special incentives that only apply to on-board bookings! For example, Princess Cruise Line Onboard Bookings usually includes both a reduced deposit and onboard credit, additionally, you didn't need a specific date picked out—as long as you made the deposit, they offer a special program called Future Cruise Credit and it is good for 4 years. Or if you had a specific date that you originally booked but, later found out couldn't make that sailing date, your deposit and onboard credit ARE TRANSFERABLE! Plus this deal IS combinable with other travel agent or cruise line promotions.

It's a win-win situation for everyone, and, should not be able to cruise at all, your deposit is refundable. While the incentives vary from cruise line to cruise line, you should feel confident booking your next cruise on-board your current cruise can only work in your favor. So, take a few minutes while on-board to take advantage of this wonderful opportunity that so few people take advantage of—you'll be glad you did!

CHAPTER 25

▼

UTTER CHAOS, THE DISEMBARKING PROCESS NOW IT'S TIME TO SAY GOOD-BYE ...

Sometime during (usually) your last full day of your cruise, more than likely the Cruise Director will have at least one member of your traveling attend a meeting about the disembarking (leaving) process. You'll be told the procedure and how to fill out your Custom's Forms, and, it will be made to sound like a very simple process. So, with a heavy heart, you leave the meeting to enjoy your last day on the ship. You'll say good-bye to your newly made friends like your table-mates and you'll try to figure out how to take your cabin attendant home with you. You finish packing, fill out your forms, and, put your luggage outside your cabin as requested and go to bed ...

When you wake up, you're going to notice something is VERY different. You put on your brave face and head out to go to breakfast ... this is probably when you'll realize just how different today is for you. Unlike other days, you're going to see people running up and down hallways (these are usually family members or friends who have traveled together checking in with each other and making sure everyone has everything they need). The cabin attendants are already in the halls with their carts ready to take on the next empty room, but, you tend to ignore it. (Partly because you want to deny that you're going home today.)

So, you head down to breakfast, if you're lucky the dining room will be open, but, more than likely you'll be sent to the buffet ... thus, it begins, the free-for-all, mass chaos known as disembarking day. You'll see more people in the buffet area than you ever realized where on the ship ... Chances are they'll be out of tea or coffee or both and it will be a wait until the next pot is brewed. Finding a table is next to impossible and, unlike other days, when they run out of something, that's it. More than likely it won't be put out again. Resigned to your fate, you take your bagel and coffee back to your cabin because there wasn't a chair to be found empty in the buffet area.

You walk into your cabin, stunned, that the cabin attendant already has cleaned the room and has it prepped for the next set of guests. Then, if it has hasn't happened already, your Cruise Director will come on the loudspeaker with those famous words "Good Morning Everyone" ... and then it starts, the Cruise Director will begin calling passengers for a variety of reasons ... sometimes it's for immigration purposes, sometimes it's to settle their onboard accounts, and sometimes it's something else all together. This goes on nearly continuously until you're ready to find the passengers and drag them down to the Guest Relations Desk yourself!

Finally, just when you didn't think you could stand another moment, the Cruise Director calls for the first set of passengers to leave. Now, this is the most frustrating part of all ... Most cruise lines offer priority boarding and leaving to frequent guests of the cruise line and those in suites ... ok, no problem, I can easily accept that—they've either paid for it or earned it and, it's their right. Sometimes those with extremely early flights (often those who have booked their own air transportation and have cut it way too close for comfort) are part of this first group.

For the rest of us ... there is no rhyme or reason on how they disembark the passengers from the ship. I've been on cruises where they'll let passenger leave according to deck level, luggage tag colors, luggage numbers and the list just goes on and on ... And, the only thing you can do is wait ... You might want to keep a deck of cards or a book or magazine in your carry-on (or in this case, your carry off) bag to help pass the time. It's going to seem like it's taking forever and, it usually isn't your imagination ... for some unknown reason this is long and it's tedious.

At last you are part of the group leaving the ship and you head down the gangpank into a large warehouse type area where you'll just see luggage ... Row after row, foot after foot ... luggage.... everywhere! There will be porters and crew members to help to direct you to the GENERAL AREA of where your luggage will be located ... Finding it ... that's another story ... good luck! After spending 15 minutes looking at every piece of luggage and blaming your spouse for buying black luggage in the first place ... you find your pieces. And, then you vow to throw out your black luggage for luggage in a shocking pink color so it's easier to find ...

You collect your pieces of luggage and head off towards the custom's officers. Not once have I been stopped, not once have my bags been inspected. Hand over your custom's form and you're free to go ... provided you've met certain requirements as outlined on the Custom's Form.

> *Side Note—You'll receive your Custom's Form, luggage tags and usually a printed instruction sheet of the procedures in your cabin the day or evening before you leave the ship. This will usually include instructions and procedures if you've gone over the limits for Custom's Declarations.*

If you've driven yourself, have a family member or friend picking you up or hired a private limousine service, the next step is as simple as finding your car, putting your luggage in and leaving. Sigh.

If you've taken advantage of cruise line offered transfers ... again ... be ready for some confusion and be ready to wait.

After you've been through Customs (or walked through and handed over your piece of paper—which is usually the case), there will be cruise line representatives directing you to various buses to take you to the airport. *I cannot stress this enough ... do not board the bus unless you've personally witnessed your luggage being placed on that same bus!*

If you don't … it could be days before your luggage finally catches up to you at home!!
And, don't be surprised if the bus does not leave until it's completely full … With that
you're off to the airport and your flight home …

So, that's pretty much what to expect as you leave the ship. It's never a pleasant
feeling but, more than likely, if you're like me, by the time you reach home,
you're already thinking about the *next* cruise.…

CHAPTER 26

▼

ON-BOARD CHARGES

While your cruise is paid approximately 85% in advance, more than likely you're going on encounter some onboard expenses like alcoholic drinks and soda-pop, gambling in the casino or playing bingo, tipping, shore tours, and purchases in the shops found on-board ... which will all go on your on-board account. In other words, cruising isn't a pay as you go system. Instead, when you board, you're given a card that is the size and shape of a credit card. This card is your ID, your room key and your onboard charge card. So, you want to buy a beer? You turn over the card and it's charged to your room. Want to buy a shirt with the cruise line logo on it? You turn over the card and it's charged to your room. I think you get the idea.

Your onboard charge card is secured with a credit card or debit card such as VISA or MasterCard or you can put down cash. All three ways (charge card, debit card, and cash) are accepted on all major cruise lines.

The tough part is telling people how much to expect to spend on their onboard account. Heavy drinkers are often shocked when they receive their end of cruise statement and it's well into the hundreds of dollars ... trust me, there is at least one on every cruise! So, to help you estimate your spending while on-board there ship, here is a list ... well at least a list of everything I could think of ... that will or could be charged to your on-board account:

- **Tips** (gratuities). The latest trend which has been in place for a few years now is automatic tipping. In other words, in days gone by, it was customary to give the people who worked hard for you during your cruise, such as your waiter, assistant waiter, and cabin attendant a gratuity for their services. Often times people didn't tip them at all and, since this is major part of their salaries, the cruise line decided that automatic tipping would help to discourage this practice of non-tipping. While you can still remove tips (and that does remain your right) or increase them if you had outstanding service, you can expect to see this expense on your end of cruise bill which will be charged to your credit card or withdrawn from your debit card or cash reserve. What needs to be understood is that if you see recommended tips are $68 per guest for the week … that goes for every single person in the cabin INCLUDING children. So if the recommended tip is $68 per guest, a family of four can expect to be charged $272 for a week's worth of service. Which roughly breaks down to $9.71 (US Dollars) per day, which is split between your waiter, assistant waiter, cabin attendant, etc.

- **Drinks**. There are some drinks such as tea, ice tea, coffee and sometimes juices that are complimentary on most of the major cruise lines. Everything else is going to be charged. So from bottled water to ginger ale to cola to beer to mixed drinks and wine … expect a charge. Pricing varies greatly but, on average you can expect soda-pop to run between $1.50—$3.00 (depending on the cruise line) per glass or can; beer runs between $4.00—$6.00 (again depending on the cruise line) per glass or can or bottle; and wine, figure $4 per glass and up. There are some cruise lines, usually, the more upscale cruise lines that include drinks in their prices but, if your traveling on the mainstream cruise lines like Carnival, Celebrity, Disney, Holland America, NCL, Princess and Royal Caribbean … you're going to be charged for these drinks. Only you know what you drink and how much … budget accordingly.

- **Gambling**. I don't think anyone out there expects this to be free, so, again, you know your habits in gambling situations…. use your own judgment and budget accordingly.

- **Shore Tours**—Depending on the cruise line, chances are your shore tours (sightseeing and activities in the various ports of call) are not going to be included with your cruise fare. Some cruise lines allow you to book and pay for your shore tours prior to coming aboard and others simply allow you to reserve them and then you pay for them once you're on board. Of course, you can wait and book on-board too. Shore tour prices vary greatly, so, check with your individual cruise line for pricing.

- **On-board Shopping**. You're going to have the opportunity to purchase many trinkets and items on-board your cruise ship. Some of the more common things you're going to find will be "An Inch of Gold" or "An Inch of Silver" where they sell an inch of gold or inch of silver starting at $1 per inch. Of course, you have the on-board shops which will sell everything from sunscreen to cruise line logo shirts to liquor to magazines. These things add up quickly, and, expect to pay premium prices on most items. One trick … if you want things like logo shirts, wait until the very end of the cruise … that's when everything goes on sale!

- **Unforeseen Expenses**—Most of the newer, larger mega ship now offer alternative restaurants on-board. These restaurants are usually an outstanding value for the quality of food and service, however, just be prepared to pay extra for it. The average alternative restaurant runs about $20 per person. Spa Services and the Beauty Salon services never come cheap on land, so, don't expect any discounts while at sea … figure the pricing to be about the same as you'd pay in any major city. Another new trend is to add Coffee House type areas on the ship. You can expect to pay premium prices for your latte and they often have pastries and cakes for purchase at these stands as well. Another money pit is the game room … I was on a Carnival ship in Europe in 2005 with one of my closest friends and her then 16 year old son. I went into the game room with him for a while and we played air hockey and several video games and within an hour, I dropped $40 without a sweat … so unless you have deep pockets, encourage your children to save and bring their own money along for the game room … and help them out by budgeting them an allowance each day.

I'm sure I'm forgetting to list a few things but these are the major expenses you'll have to plan for while on a cruise vacation. And, believe it or not, even with all of these "extras" factored in … a cruise vacation is still one of the best values for your money in today's vacation market!

CHAPTER 27

▼

CRUISE TERMINALS
IN THE UNITED STATES

This chapter is dedicated to listing addresses, parking and directions to the major passenger ship cruise terminals located throughout the United States. They are listed in alphabetical order by city name. Only ports where embarking or disembarking take place are listed. *The information contained is deemed accurate at the time of press in 2007.*

Baltimore	Mobile
Bayonne	New Orleans
Boston	New York
Brooklyn	Norfolk
Charleston	Philadelphia
Fort Lauderdale	Port Canaveral
Galveston	San Deigo
Honolulu	San Francisco
Los Angeles	Seattle
Miami	Tampa

BALTIMORE, Maryland

2001 E. McComas Street Baltimore, MD 21230
http://www.marylandports.com/cruises/index.htm

Directions
From points South:
Follow I-95 North to Exit 55, Key Highway. From the ramp, stay straight on East McComas Street.
The South Locust Point Cruise Terminal's entrance is on the right.
From points North:
Follow I-95 South through the Ft. McHenry Tunnel, be sure to be in the right lane when going through the tunnel. Take Exit 55, Key Highway. Turn left at the traffic light onto East McComas Street. Follow the signs to the South Locust Point Cruise Terminal's entrance on the right.
Parking as of 2006
No advance reservations are required to park in the secure lot located on the South Locust Point Marine Terminal. Ample long-term parking is located within walking distance of the Passenger Building and courtesy/handicap shuttles are available. Parking fees are payable upon arrival by cash or traveler's checks only.

Passenger Cars—$10.00 per day
Recreational Vehicles—$20.00 per day
Busses—$25.00 per day
Upon arrival, passengers will drop off their luggage into the assigned containers. Please make sure to have your cruise line issued luggage tags filled out and attached to your bags before entering the facility. After dropping off your luggage, you will then proceed to the long-term parking lot.

BAYONNE, New Jersey

Peninsula at Bayonne
Bayonne, NJ 07002
http://www.cruiseliberty.com/

- From Northern New Jersey

  Take the New Jersey Turnpike South to Exit 14A (Bayonne). After tollbooth, follow signs for Route 440 South. Proceed 1 1/2 miles to Terminal on your left.

- From Connecticut—near I-95

  Take I-95 south into New York State. Continue on I-95 to and over the George Washington Bridge. Follow signs for New Jersey Turnpike and proceed South to Exit 14A (Bayonne). After tollbooth, follow signs for Route 440 South. Proceed 1 1/2 miles to Terminal on your left.

- From Connecticut—near I-84

  Take I-84 West into New York State. Take I-684 South to I-287 West to I-87 South. Follow signs to and over the George Washington Bridge. Follow signs for the New Jersey Turnpike South. Continue to Exit 14A (Bayonne). After tollbooth, follow signs for Route 440 South. Proceed 1 1/2 miles to Terminal on your left.

- From Westchester County

  Take I-684 South to I-287 West to I-87 South. Follow signs to and over the George Washington Bridge. Follow signs for the New Jersey Turnpike South. Continue to Exit 14A (Bayonne). After tollbooth, follow signs for Route 440 South. Proceed 1 1/2 miles to Terminal on your left.

- From Rockland County

  Take the Palisades Parkway South to I-80 West. Follow signs for the New Jersey Turnpike South. Continue to Exit 14A (Bayonne). After tollbooth, follow signs for Route 440 South. Proceed 1 1/2 miles to Terminal on your left.

- From The Bronx

Proceed to and across the George Washington Bridge. Follow signs for the New Jersey Turnpike South. Continue to Exit 14A (Bayonne). After tollbooth, follow signs for Route 440 South. Proceed 1 1/2 miles to Terminal on your left.

- From Manhattan

Proceed to and through the Lincoln Tunnel. Follow I-495 West to the New Jersey Turnpike. Proceed South to Exit 14A (Bayonne).

After tollbooth, follow signs for Route 440 South. Proceed 1 1/2 miles to Terminal on your left.

- From Brooklyn or Queens

Enter Manhattan using the closest bridge or tunnel. Proceed crosstown to and through the Lincoln Tunnel. Follow I-495 West to the New Jersey Turnpike. Proceed South to Exit 14A (Bayonne). After tollbooth, follow signs for Route 440 South. Proceed 1 1/2 miles to Terminal on your left.

- From Staten Island

Take Route 440 North to and over the Bayonne Bridge. Continue on Route 440, 1 1/2 miles to Terminal on your right.

- From Southern New Jersey—Shore Points

Take the Garden State Parkway North to Exit 129 (New Jersey Turnpike). Continue North on the New Jersey Turnpike to Exit 14A (Bayonne). After tollbooth, follow signs for Route 440 South. Proceed 1 1/2 miles to Terminal on your left.

Parking as of 2006

The parking facility will be located adjacent to the cruise terminal. The parking facility will only accept cash on arrival and will not accept credit cards or checks—$15 per day. The on-site parking facility is secured and will be large enough to accommodate all guests who choose to park their cars at the pier.

BOSTON, Massachusetts

One Black Falcon Avenue
Boston, Massachusetts 02210

http://www.massport.com/ports/cruis.html

From the North (coming south on I93):
On the expressway downtown, inside the Liberty Tunnel, take Exit #23 (Purchase Street). At the top of the ramp, go to the traffic signal, and turn left onto Seaport Boulevard. Continue on Seaport Boulevard to the fifth traffic light (this is where Seaport Blvd becomes Northern Ave). Continue straight into the Boston Marine Industrial Park, following Northern Avenue to the end where you take a right onto Tide Street, and an immediate left onto Drydock Avenue. Follow Drydock Avenue as it turns right at the end of the Boston Design Center. Turn right again onto Black Falcon Avenue, traveling straight to the stop sign, where you will be directed by Port Officers for either passenger drop-off or to the parking garage.

From the South:
Take I-93 north to Boston, take (new) Exit 20 to I-90 east/Logan Airport. You will travel into a new tunnel toward Logan. Inside the tunnel, take Exit 25/South Boston. At the traffic lights, you will be at Congress Street. Continue forward onto East Service Drive. At the next signal, turn right onto Seaport Boulevard. Continue straight onto Northern Avenue and proceed into the Marine Industrial Park. Continue to the end and turn right onto Tide Street and an immediate left onto Drydock Avenue. Follow Drydock Avenue as it turns right at the end of the Boston Design Center. Turn right again onto Black Falcon Avenue, traveling straight to the stop sign, where you will be directed by Port Officers for either passenger drop-off or to the parking garage.

From the West (Mass. Turnpike, I-90 Eastbound):
Follow the Mass. Pike east toward Logan Airport. Pass the I-90/I-93 interchange and enter a tunnel eastbound. In the tunnel, take Exit 25/South Boston. At the traffic lights, you will be at Congress Street. Continue forward onto B Street. At the next signal, turn right onto Seaport Boulevard. Continue straight onto Northern Avenue and proceed into the Marine Industrial Park. Continue to the end and turn right onto Tide Street and an immediate left onto Drydock Avenue.

Follow Drydock Avenue as it turns right at the end of the Boston Design Center. Turn right again onto Black Falcon Avenue, traveling straight to the stop sign, where you will be directed by Port Officers for either passenger drop-off or to the parking garage.

From Logan Airport (TW Tunnel, Mass. Turnpike, I-90 Westbound):
Follow signs for the Ted Williams Tunnel ($3 toll). From the right lane, take the first exit—Exit 25/South Boston. At the traffic lights, you will be at Congress Street. Continue forward onto B Street. At the next signal, turn right onto Seaport Boulevard. Continue straight onto Northern Avenue and proceed into the Marine Industrial Park. Continue to the end and turn right onto Tide Street and an immediate left onto Drydock Avenue. Follow Drydock Avenue as it turns right at the end of the Boston Design Center. Turn right again onto Black Falcon Avenue, traveling straight to the stop sign, where you will be directed by Port Officers for either passenger drop-off or to the parking garage.

Public Transportation:
Public transportation is available via the Silver Line Waterfront bus. For more information on fares and schedules, call 1 (800) 392-6100 or check the MBTA website (www.mbta.com).

Parking for the cruise season is generally available at the EDIC (Economic Development Industrial Corporation) garage, a five-story, indoor parking facility owned by the City of Boston and operated by EDIC. It is located across from the Black Falcon Cruise Terminal. Rates are $14 per day and cash, Visa, or MasterCard are accepted. AMPLE PARKING—NO RESERVATIONS REQUIRED. In the event that long-term parking is not available in the garage, Massport will direct passengers to an alternative parking location when you arrive at the terminal. For further information about parking at the Boston Marine Industrial Park, please call 617.918.6225 (option 3)

Please note: cruise passengers pay for parking when entering the garage. Follow signs for cruise parking to a toll booth attendant who will issue a decal to indicate you've paid in advance.

BROOKLYN (Red Hook), New York

Pier 12, Building 112
Brooklyn, NY 11231
http://www.nycruiseterminal.com/terminalBKN.html

DIRECTIONS
To Brooklyn Terminal—
From Manhattan via Battery Tunnel:
From Manhattan, take the Battery Tunnel (I-478-E) into Brooklyn. Continue onto the westbound Brooklyn-Queens Expressway (I-278-W) and immediately take the first exit on the right: Exit 26- Hamilton Avenue onto the service road. Stay to the left and make a left-U-turn at the intersection of Hamilton Avenue with Clinton Street/9th Street, then continue west along the westbound Hamilton Avenue service road. Continue on the service road to its end at Van Brunt Street. Turn left at Van Brunt Street, travel 2 blocks and then turn right onto Bowne Street to enter the terminal.

From Manhattan via the Brooklyn or Manhattan Bridges and from La Guardia Airport (LGA):
From the Brooklyn and Manhattan Bridges, or LaGuardia Airport, get onto the westbound Brooklyn-Queens Expressway (I-278-W) and take Exit 26—Hamilton Avenue onto the service road. Stay to the left and make a left-U-turn at the intersection of Hamilton Avenue with Clinton Street/9th Street, then continue west along the westbound Hamilton Avenue service road. Continue on the service road to its end at Van Brunt Street. Turn left at Van Brunt Street, travel 2 blocks and then turn right onto Bowne Street to enter the terminal.

From John F. Kennedy (JFK) Airport:
From John F. Kennedy Airport, get onto the eastbound Brooklyn-Queens Expressway (I-278-E) to Exit 26-Hamilton Avenue. After exit, continue along westbound Hamilton Avenue service road. Continue on the service road to its end at Van Brunt Street. Turn left at Van Brunt Street, travel 2 blocks and then turn right onto Bowne Street.

From Long Island:
From Long Island, take the LIE west to the westbound Brooklyn-Queens Expressway (I-278-W, just after Exit 18 Maurice Avenue) and take Exit 26—

Hamilton Avenue onto the service road. Stay to the left and make a left-U-turn at the intersection of Hamilton Avenue with Clinton Street/9th Street, then continue west along the westbound Hamilton Avenue service road. Continue on the service road to its end at Van Brunt Street. Turn left at Van Brunt Street, travel 2 blocks and then turn right onto Bowne Street to enter the terminal.

From Queens:
Westbound Brooklyn-Queens Expressway (I-278-W) and take Exit 26—Hamilton Avenue onto the service road. Hamilton Avenue onto the service road. Stay to the left and make a left-U-turn at the intersection of Hamilton Avenue with Clinton Street/9th Street, then continue west along the westbound Hamilton Avenue service road. Continue on the service road to its end at Van Brunt Street. Turn left at Van Brunt Street, travel 2 blocks and then turn right onto Bowne Street to enter the terminal.

From New Jersey:
South New Jersey:
NJ Turnpike; south on Turnpike to Exit 13; cross Goethals Bridge to I-278, Staten Island Expressway and cross Verrazano Bridge into Brooklyn. Continue north on Gowanus/BQE and exit at Exit 26 (Hamilton Avenue), After Exit, go down the ramp to Van Brunt Street to its end, make a left turn on Van Brunt and travel 2 blocks and turn right onto Bowne Street to enter terminal.
West New Jersey:
I-78 East to NJ Turnpike to Exit 13; cross Goethals Bridge to I-278, Staten Island Expressway and cross Verrazano Bridge into Brooklyn. Continue north on Gowanus/BQE and exit at Exit 26 (Hamilton Avenue), After Exit, go down the ramp to Van Brunt Street to its end, make a left turn on Van Brunt and travel 2 blocks and turn right onto Bowne Stet to enter terminal.
North New Jersey:
East on I-80 to I-280. Take I-280 east to NJ Turnpike. Travel south on Turnpike to Exit 13. cross Goethals Bridge, then proceed as above.

From Newark International Airport (EWR):
From EWR via Battery Tunnel:
From Newark International Airport (EWR), take the US-1-9 ramp toward RT-21/Newark Downtown/US-22/I-78. Merge onto US-1 &9 N/US-9 N/US-1 N, which becomes 12th Street. Follow 12th Street, pay the portions toll at Boyle Plaza, and continue to the Holland Tunnel into Manhattan.

Toll for entering Manhattan is $6 by cash, $4 EZ Pass off-peak, and $5 EZ Pass peak. Take Exit 1 towards Route 9A/West Side Highway/West St, take a slight left onto Laight Street, then take a left onto Route 9A/West Side Highway and continue south. Take the Battery Tunnel (Exit 2) towards I-278/Brooklyn. Continue onto the westbound Brooklyn-Queens Expressway (I-278-W) and immediately take the first exit on the right: Exit 26- Hamilton Avenue onto the service road. Stay to the left and make a left-U-turn at the intersection of Hamilton Avenue with Clinton Street/9th Street, then continue west along the westbound Hamilton Avenue service road. Continue on the service road to its end at Van Brunt Street. Turn left at Van Brunt Street, travel 2 blocks and then turn right onto Bowne Street to enter the terminal.

From EWR via the Brooklyn Bridge:
From Newark International Airport (EWR), take the US-1-9 ramp toward RT-21/Newark Downtown/US-22/I-78. Merge onto US-1 &9 N/US-9 N/US-1 N, which becomes 12th Street. Follow 12th Street, pay the portions toll at Boyle Plaza, and continue to the Holland Tunnel into Manhattan.

Toll for entering Manhattan is $6 by cash, $4 EZ Pass off-peak, and $5 EZ Pass peak. Take Exit 3 towards Brooklyn, taking a left onto Beach Street/Ericsson Street. Stay right on Beach Street, which becomes Walker Street, and take a right onto Lafayette Street. Lafayette Street becomes Centre Street, and merge onto the Brooklyn Bridge via the ramp on the left. Take the Cadman Plaza W exit ramp towards I-278W/Brooklyn-Queens Expressway and take Exit 26—Hamilton Avenue onto the service road. Stay to the left and make a left-U-turn at the intersection of Hamilton Avenue with Clinton Street/9th Street, then continue west along the westbound Hamilton Avenue service road. Continue on the service road to its end at Van Brunt Street. Turn left at Van Brunt Street, travel 2 blocks and then turn right onto Bowne Street to enter the terminal.

From EWR via the Manhattan Bridge:
From Newark International Airport (EWR), take the US-1-9 ramp toward RT-21/Newark Downtown/US-22/I-78. Merge onto US-1 &9 N/US-9 N/US-1 N, which becomes 12th Street. Follow 12th Street, pay the portions toll at Boyle Plaza, and continue to the Holland Tunnel into Manhattan.

Toll for entering Manhattan is $6 by cash, $4 EZ Pass off-peak, and $5 EZ Pass peak. Take Exit 1 towards Route 9A/West Side Highway/West St, take a slight left onto Laight Street, and continue onto Canal Street.

Continue west along Canal Street, and merge onto the Manhattan Bridge on-ramp. Take the off-ramp towards I-278W/Brooklyn-Queens Expressway and take Exit 26—Hamilton Avenue onto the service road. Stay to the left and make a left-U-turn at the intersection of Hamilton Avenue with Clinton Street/9th Street, then continue west along the westbound Hamilton Avenue service road. Continue on the service road to its end at Van Brunt Street. Turn left at Van Brunt Street, travel 2 blocks and then turn right onto Bowne Street to enter the terminal.

From Brooklyn Terminal—
To Manhattan via the Brooklyn and Manhattan Bridges and to LaGuardia Airport:
From terminal exit, continue east along Bowne Street and merge with Hamilton Avenue service road. Stay left and merge left onto underpass at Columbia Street, follow road and merge onto the eastbound Brooklyn-Queens Expressway (I-278-E) and continue to exits 28B (Brooklyn Bridge), 29A (Manhattan Bridge), or continue on I-278-E as it turns into the Grand Central Parkway into Queens. Take Exit 5 to the LaGuardia Marine Air Terminal or Exit 7 to the main terminal.

To Manhattan via the Battery Tunnel:
From Terminal exit, continue east along Bowne Street and merge with the eastbound Hamilton Avenue service road. Stay left and make the left-U-turn at 9th Street/Clinton Street, continuing westbound along the Hamilton Avenue Service Road. Stay left and merge onto the Battery Tunnel access toll road.

To John F. Kennedy (JFK) Airport:
From Terminal exit, continue east along Bowne Street and merge with the eastbound Hamilton Avenue service road. Stay left and make the immediate left merge onto the westbound Brooklyn-Queens Expressway (I-278-W) at Columbia Street. Continue on I-278-W to Exit 16-Belt Parkway. Continue on Belt Parkway to Exit 19-John F. Kennedy Airport.
Parking

Parking at the Brooklyn Cruise Terminal is about 200-300 yards south of the terminal entrance/exit. Parking resides in an outdoor lot with security. Handicap spaces are available and the same rates apply as follows.

Parking Rates
Daily Rate (10 Hours)
$19.00

Overnight Rate (24 Hours)
$20.00

Day Rate (multi days)
$18.00

Short Term 20 minute Parking
$6.00

For inquiries regarding Brooklyn Cruise Terminal parking, please contact:
Donovan Withers
By email: dwithers@impark.com
By phone: (212) 686-4548

CHARLESTON, South Carolina

196 Concord Street
Charleston, South Carolina 29401
http://www.scspa.com/cruises/cruises.asp

Directions
Traveling from I-95 North or South—
* Take I-26 (S.E.) toward Charleston
* Exit at East Bay Street
* Turn left on to Market Street
* Turn right on to Concord Street
* The driveway to the Cruise Ship Terminal will be on the left

Traveling from US Highway 17—
* Take US Highway 17 toward Charleston
* Exit at East Bay Street and turn right off the exit ramp
* Turn left on to Market Street
* Turn right on to Concord Street
* The driveway to the Cruise Ship Terminal will be on the left

Parking
$8.00 per day (rate subject to change by the Port Authority)
* Secured, outdoor parking
* No advance reservations required
* RVs will be charges per parking space
* Shuttle service available to/from the terminal/parking lot

FORT LAUDERDALE, Florida

Fort Lauderdale, Florida 33316

http://www.broward.org/port/cruise.htm

Main Enterance—Take I-595 East straight into the Port (I-595 becomes Eller Drive once inside the Port). I-595 runs east/west with connections to the Fort Lauderdale/Hollywood International Airport, U.S.1, I-95, State Road 7 (441), Florida s Turnpike, Sawgrass Expressway and I-75.
North Enterance—Take U.S.1 or A1A to 17th Street Causeway in Fort Lauderdale and turn south onto Eisenhower Blvd.
US1/Federal Highway Enterance—At the intersection of State Road 84 East and U.S.1 (Federal Hwy.), turn east into the seaport.

Parking
All parking facilities charge $2 for 0-1 hour, $5 for 1-5 hours, and then $1 per hour thereafter up to a maximum daily fee of $12. Convenient parking for cruise passengers is available in the Northport or Midport Parking Garage. Garages are security-patrolled, and provide handicapped parking with unimpeded access to crosswalks and elevators.

GALVESTON, Texas

2502 Harborside Drive
Galveston, Texas 77550
http://www.portofgalveston.com/cruiseinformation/

Directions
From the North and West:
Harborside Drive (State Highway 275):
I-45 South to Galveston Island
From right lane on Causeway, take Exit 1C
Exit 1C Feeder Road to Harborside Drive (Hwy 275)
Turn left (north) on to Harborside Drive
Continue 4.7 miles to Kempner/22nd Street
Turn left on Kempner/22nd Street to Cruise Terminal
From the East:
State Highway 87—West to Galveston Island using Vehicle Ferry System
Exit Ferry on to Ferry Road/Hwy 87
Continue Ferry Road to Harborside Drive
Turn right (west) on Harborside Drive
Continue approximately 20 city blocks
Turn right on Kempner/22nd Street to Cruise Terminal

For passenger convenience, safety and best service, the Port of Galveston encourages cruise visitors to proceed directly to the cruise terminal complex to drop-off luggage and passengers. Porters are available to assist with luggage tags and directions to the parking lots, beginning the embarkation process. A free shuttle will return you to the terminal.

Parking
Port of Galveston Official Parking Lot Long-Term Rates

• 4-Day Cruise: $40

• 5-Day Cruise: $45

• 7-Day Cruise: $60

• 10-Day Cruise: $75

- 11-Day Cruise: $80

- 12-Day Cruise: $85

Note: The above charges for parking apply to vehicles occupying a single standard car parking space. Vehicles, such as buses or large campers, occupying two or more parking spaces will be charged double the above rates. Cash, Travelers Checks and Credit Cards (Visa and MasterCard) are accepted at Port of Galveston Official Parking Lots.

HONOLULU, Hawaii

1 Aloha Tower Dr
Honolulu, Hawaii 96813

http://www.hawaii.gov/dot/harbors/oahu/oahu.htm

The Aloha Tower Marketplace (Port of Honolulu) is located 5.4 miles from the Honolulu International Airport. There is no parking information available at this time.

LOS ANGELES (San Pedro), California

425 S. Palos Verdes Street
San Pedro, California 90731

http://www.portoflosangeles.org/recreation_Cruising.htm

DIRECTIONS:
The World Cruise Center at the Port of Los Angeles in San Pedro is approximately
18 miles (29 kilometers) south of Los Angeles International Airport (LAX), 25
miles (40 kilometers) south of downtown Los Angeles and 10 miles (16 kilometers)
west of Long Beach, with easy freeway access from both directions.

From LAX: Travel southbound on the San Diego Freeway (Interstate 405), then
southbound on the Harbor Freeway (Interstate 110). Exit at Harbor Boulevard
and proceed straight through the Harbor Boulevard intersection. Turn right to
enter the World Cruise Center.
From downtown Los Angeles: Travel southbound on the Harbor Freeway (Interstate 110). Exit at Harbor Boulevard and proceed straight through the Harbor
Boulevard intersection. Turn right to enter the World Cruise Center.
From Long Beach: Travel westbound on Ocean Boulevard, Seaside Avenue and
the Vincent Thomas Bridge (State Highway 47). Exit at Harbor Boulevard and
proceed straight through the Harbor Boulevard intersection. Turn right to enter
the World Cruise Center.

Parking
Overnight parking is available and no reservations are required. Most lots are
open seven days/week, 24 hours/day. Courtesy shuttles are provided to and from
the cruise terminal on scheduled ship days. Shuttles are not wheelchair accessible.
Parking rates are $1 each hour for the first 10 hours, with a $12 daily maximum.
Cash, Travelers Checks, and Credit Cards are accepted. For more information,
call Parking Concepts at 1-800-540-PARK.

MIAMI, Florida

1741 Africa Way Dodge Island
Miami, Florida 33132
http://www.miamidade.gov/portofmiami/cruise.asp

DIRECTIONS
Take I-95 north or south to I-395. Follow the directional signs to the Biscayne Boulevard exit. When you get to Biscayne Blvd., make a right. Go to 5th Street which converts to Port Blvd. (landmark: American Airlines Basketball Arena) make a left and go over the Port bridge. Follow directional signs to designated terminal.

Parking:
Facilities are available at all terminals for the parking of vehicles for passengers boarding ships and for Port visitors at rates designated by the Seaport Director.

Parking for cruise passengers is $12 per day. Parking for visitors is $5 per day. Cash or credit cards are accepted (Visa or Master Card only).

Parking for oversized vehicles is approximately $24 per day.
(depending on overall dimensions)

All established parking rates will be posted at each facility and applied to the day a vehicle enters the parking lot and to each succeeding day it remains on the lot.

Credit card payments are only accepted at Parking Garage # 5 and Parking Garage # 6.
**Only Visa and Master Card are accepted.

MOBILE, Alabama

Alabama State Docks
Intersection of Beauregard Road and Water Street
Mobile, AL

http://www.shipmobile.com/

Directions
From I-65 North or South—
* Take I-65 to I-165
* Exit at Water Street
* Directional signage will be visible
* Security Check-In will take place at the Hank Aaron Loop. All guests will be pre-screened before proceeding to the parking lot and cruise terminal.

From I-10 East or West—
* Exit at Water Street
* Directional signage will be visible
* Security Check-In will take place at the Hank Aaron Loop. All guests will be pre-screened before proceeding to the parking lot and cruise terminal.

Parking
$7.00 per day (rate subject to change by the Port Authority)
* Secured, outdoor parking
* No advance reservations required
* RVs will be charged per parking space
* Cash only; prepay prior to the cruise

NEW ORLEANS, Louisiana

Two Julia Street
New Orleans, Louisiana 70130
http://www.portno.com/cruise_info.htm

DIRECTIONS

- FROM CENTRAL BUSINESS DISTRICT: Convention Center Blvd. to Henderson St., left on Henderson St. continue to Port of New Orleans Place, left on Port of New Orleans Place to Julia St. Terminals 1 and 2 or right to Delta Queen (Robin St. Wharf).

- FROM INTERSTATE 10 (EAST OR WEST): Exit at Business 90W/Westbank (locally known as Pontchartrain Expressway). Proceed to Tchoupitoulas St./South Peters St. exit, continue to Convention Center Blvd., right on Convention Center Blvd. continue to Henderson St., left on Henderson St. continue to Port of New Orleans Place, left on Port of New Orleans Place to Julia St. Terminals 1 and 2 or right to Delta Queen (Robin St. Wharf).

- FROM RIVER BOUND PONTCHARTRAIN EXPRESSWAY: Exit at Tchoupitoulas St./South Peters St. exit, continue to Convention Center Blvd., right on Convention Center Blvd. continue to Henderson St., left on Henderson St. continue to Port of New Orleans Place, left on Port of New Orleans Place to Julia St. Terminals 1 and 2 or right to Delta Queen (Robin St. Wharf).

- FROM RIVER BOUND WESTBANK EXPRESSWAY: Westbank Expressway to Crescent City Connection, continue over Crescent City Connection, exit at Tchoupitoulas St. exit. Continue to Henderson St., left on Henderson St. continue to Port of New Orleans Place, left on Port of New Orleans Place to Julia St. Terminals 1 and 2 or right to Delta Queen (Robin St. Wharf).

- FROM NEW ORLEANS INTERNATIONAL AIRPORT: Take I-10 East toward New Orleans. Follow signs for Westbank (Business 90) as you approach downtown. Exit at Tchoupitoulas St./South Peters St. exit, continue to Convention Center Blvd., right on Convention Center Blvd. continue to Henderson St., left on Henderson St. continue to Port of New Orleans Place, left on Port of New Orleans Place to Julia St. Terminals 1 and 2 or right to Delta Queen (Robin St. Wharf).

Parking

Poydras Street Parking Lot
At the base of the Tchoupitoulas/S. Peters exit from the Pontchartrain Expressway (Exit 11C), continue to the second stop light and turn right onto Tchoupitoulas St. Go two blocks to the first stop light and turn left onto Henderson St. Go two blocks to Port of New Orleans Place, turn left and continue past the cruise terminals (after you have offloaded luggage and passengers) to the lot. This is a surface lot with approximately 75 spaces, it is fenced, lighted and patrolled. For information call (504) 528-3318
Delta Queen Steamboat Parking Instructions
At the base of the Tchoupitoulas/S. Peters exit from the Pontchartrain Expressway (Exit 11C), continue to the second stop light and turn right onto Tchoupitoulas St. Go two blocks to the first stop light and turn left onto Henderson St. Go two blocks to Port of New Orleans Place, turn right, and go into the first entrance into the terminal building on your left. For further instructions call (800)543-1949

NEW YORK, New York

Piers #88/90/92
711 12th Avenue
New York, New York 10019
http://www.nypst.com/

(For Red Hook Brooklyn, See Brooklyn, New York)

DIRECTIONS FOR PASSENGERS LEAVING OR RETURNING TO THE
MANHATTAN CRUISE TERMINAL

Passengers embarking or disembarking enter Cruise Vessels from the mid-level
Customs Hall which is reached by way of:

- the Vehicle Ramp at 55th Street;

- Elevator or Escalator from Street Level of all three Piers, at 48th, 50th or 52nd
  Street depending on location of their vessel;

- or Down Escalator from Roof Top Parking Lot.

PASSENGERS EMBARKING

From Buses:
Passengers will arrive at the Street Level of Pier where their Cruise Vessel is berthed. Busses will park either in slots at front of Pier or inside the Pier. Passengers
can access the mid-level Customs Hall via either of two large Passenger Elevators
at Street Entrance of the Piers or via Escalators which are located on South Side
of the Entrance Area of each Pier. Their baggage will be moved directly from
Busses to the Vessel. Passengers should then proceed to complete the Boarding
Process at the Embarkation Desks of the Cruise Line which are positioned inside
the Customs Hall.

From Limousines:
Passengers will be dropped by arriving Limousines in Receiving Area at Street
Level directly in front of Pier where their Cruise Vessel is berthed. They can
access the Customs Hall by using either of the two Passenger Elevators at the
head of each Pier, or use the Escalator on the South Side of the Entrance Area.

Baggage will be received by Porters directly from their Limousine and moved to the Vessel. Passengers should then proceed to complete the boarding Process at the Embarkation Desks of the Cruise Line inside the Customs Hall.

From Taxi Cabs:
Passengers arriving by Taxi will be driven up the 54th Street Viaduct Ramp to the Receiving Area adjacent to their Cruise Vessel's Berth. Their baggage will be received there by Porters and taken to the Vessel. Passengers can then transit inside the Pier to the Embarkation Desks of the Cruise Line to complete the Boarding Process.

From Private Vehicles:
Passengers arriving by Private Vehicle should drive up the 54th Street Viaduct Ramp to the Receiving Area adjacent to their Cruise Vessel's Berth. Signs identifying the Vessel are posted on pillars nearest the proper berth. Baggage will be received there by Porters and taken directly to the Vessel. Passengers can then transit inside the Pier to the Embarkation Desks of the Cruise Line to complete the Boarding Process.

PASSENGERS DISEMBARKING

Upon Returning From The Cruise:
As Passengers arrive at the Pier they enter the same Customs Hall from which they had originally embarked. Their Baggage will have been positioned by Porters under appropriate signs coded by Letter, Cabin Number or Color depending on system followed by Cruise Line. After selecting their bags they proceed past Customs Inspector and rendering their Customs Declaration assisted by Porter according to their preference.

Bus and Limousine Passengers descend to Street Level via Two Elevators or Single Escalator located at far end of Lobby.

Taxi Passengers exit Lobby Area with Baggage onto Viaduct; claim numbered ticket from Taxi Dispatcher and await Taxi Service on Sidewalk Queue Stripe.

Private Vehicle Passengers exit Lobby Area with Baggage onto Viaduct to await Driver in Party who should proceed to Rooftop Parking Area to reclaim Private Auto. Driver must exit Rooftop (3rd) Level to Ramp at North End of Roof, descend to mid (2nd) Level and proceed to locate others in Party who have remained at Disembarkation Pier with Baggage.

Exit from the Terminal is via Ramp to Street at South End of mid-Level.

Parking

Cruise Parking (Multi-Day Passengers) $24.00 Per Day

Daily Rate (Up to 10 Hours) (Drop Offs/Visitors) $22.00

Overnight Rate (per 24 Hours) $25.00

Monthly Rate (For Parking in Excess of 8 Days) $180.00

Taxes are included in the Rates.

Payment accepted in Cash or Travelers' Checks.

Visa and MasterCard Accepted.

Reservations are not accepted.

For more information call P&O Parking 212-641-4454

NORFOLK, Virginia

One Waterside Drive
Norfolk, Virginia 23510

http://www.cruisenorfolk.org/

DIRECTIONS:
Less than one mile from I-264, the Cedar Grove site is conveniently located on Monticello Avenue between Virginia Beach Boulevard and Princess Anne Road in Downtown Norfolk. From Interstate-264, take the City Hall Exit (Exit #10). At the light, turn right onto St. Paul's Boulevard and follow our "Cruise Parking" signs.

PHILADELPHIA, Pennsylvania

The Philadelphia Cruise Terminal at Pier 1
5100 South Broad Street
Philadelphia, PA
http://cruisephilly.org/

Directions
From north of Philadelphia and from New Jersey via the Ben Franklin Bridge or
the Walt Whitman Bridge:
* South on I-95
* Take Exit 17 (Broad Street)
* Make a left on to Broad Street
* Enter Main Gate at Navy Yard
* Continue on Broad Street
* The Cruise Terminal (Building #3) is the last building on the right

From south of Philadelphia and from New Jersey via the Commodore Barry
Bridge:
* North on I-95
* Take Exit 17 (Broad Street)
* Make a left at first light at bottom of ramp (Zinkoff Blvd)
* Make another left on to Broad Street and stay to the right
* Enter Main Gate at Philadelphia Naval Business Center (PNBC)
* Continue on Broad Street
* The Cruise Terminal (Building #3) is the last building on the right

From west of Philadelphia or the Pennsylvania Turnpike (Exit 24—Valley
Forge):
* Schuylkill Expressway East (I-76)
* Take I-76 East to Broad Street Exit
* Take Broad Street South to Main Gate at Navy Yard
* Continue on Broad Street
* The Cruise Terminal (Building #3) is the last building on the right

From Blue Route (I-476):
* Take I-476 to I-95 North
* Take I-95 North to Exit 17 (Broad Street)

* Make a left at first light at bottom of ramp (Zinkoff Blvd)
* Make another left on to Broad Street and stay to the right
* Enter Main Gate at Philadelphia Naval Business Center (PNBC)
* Continue on Broad Street
* The Cruise Terminal (Building #3) is the last building on the right

From Center City Philadelphia:
* Take Broad Street South to Main Gate at the Navy Yard
* Continue on Broad Street
* The Cruise Terminal (Building #3) is the last building on the right

Travel Time: Approximately 30 minutes from the Philadelphia International Airport.

Parking
$60.00 flat fee per passenger vehicle (rate subject to change by the Port Authority)
* Covered garage (located a few blocks from the terminal)
* No advance reservations required
* $100.00 flat fee for two axle multi-passenger vehicle
* Shuttle service available to/from the terminal/parking garage
* Cash only: prepay prior to the cruise

PORT CANAVERAL, Florida

North Terminal
1492 Charles M. Rowland Drive
Port Canaveral, FL

Directions
From I-95 North/South—
* Take Exit 77-A East—Beeline Expressway (528 East)
* Take exit for North Terminal
* Follow signs for Pier #5—North Terminal

From Orlando International Airport—
* Take Beeline Expressway (528 East)
* Take exit for North Terminal
* Follow signs for Pier #5—North Terminal

From Tampa—
* Take I-4 East
* Exit at Beeline Expressway (528 East)
* Take exit for North Terminal
* Follow signs for Pier #5—North Terminal

Travel Time: 45 miles from the Orlando International Airport; travel time is approximately 50 minutes.

Parking
$8.00 per day (rate subject to change by Port Authority)
* Guarded, outdoor parking lot
* No advance reservations required
* RVs will pay for two spaces

SAN DIEGO, California

3165 Pacific Highway
San Diego, CA 92101-1128
Main Phone: (619) 686-6200

http://www.portofsandiego.org/sandiego_maritime/cruise/

DIRECTIONS:
Driving South on Interstate 5: Take I-5 into downtown San Diego. Exit Sassafras (airport exit). Proceed straight on exit road, which turns into India, until Laurel. Turn right on Laurel and proceed west until Harbor Drive. Make a left on Harbor Drive. From that point, the cruise ship terminal is approximately ¼ of a mile on the right.

Driving North on Interstate 5: Take I-5 into downtown San Diego. Exit Hawthorn (airport exit). Hawthorn steers west toward the San Diego Bay waterfront and Harbor Drive. At Harbor Drive, make a left. From that point, the cruise ship terminal is approximately ¼ of a mile on the right.

Parking:
Parking, long term and daily, is available at the lane field facility located on Broadway between Pacific Highway and North Harbor Drive. The rate is $12.00 a day and space is limited. Central Parking, operator of the parking lot may be contacted at (619) 235-5690.

Long-term parking is also available at Park & Ride lots near the Terminal. They service both the Cruise Ship Terminal and the Airport. Rates vary from $9.00-17.00 per day and may include secured, covered parking. Shuttle service is available at no charge. Please consult the local phone book under "Parking Lots & Garages" to contact operators.

SAN FRANCISCO, California

The Embarcadero
San Francisco, CA 94111
Main Phone: 415-274-0400

http://www.sfmerchants.com/cruise_terminal/
san_francisco_cruise_terminal.htm

DIRECTIONS:

From the South Bay: Take Highway 101 North to Highway 80 East, exit at 4th Street, stay left onto Bryant Street (get in right land) stay on Bryant Street to Embarcadero. Turn left onto Embarcadero (get into right lane) go straight about 2 1-2 miles. Look for signs for the Pier.

From North Bay: Take Highway 101 South across the Golden Gate Bridge, pass through the toll plaza and stay on your left, take Lombard Street to Van Ness Ave., take a left onto Van Ness Ave (stay right), follow Van Ness Avenue to Bay Street (about 3 blocks), stay on Bay Street until it runs into Embarcadero, turn let onto Embarcadero, look for signs for the Pier.

From the East Bay: Take Interstate 80 West across the Bay Bridge, Take the Harrison Embarcadero Exit (on left side), turn right at Harrison St. (end of off-ramp), follow Harrison to Embarcadero, turn left onto Embarcadero, go straight and look for signs for the Pier, approximately 2 miles.

Parking
Approximately $9.00 per day (rates subject to change by the Port Authority)

SEATTLE, Washington

Bell St. Pier
2203 Alaskan Way
Seattle, WA 98121

http://www.portseattle.org/seaport/cruise/

Directions
Merge onto WA-518 E. Take the I-5 north exit on the left toward Seattle. Merge onto I-5 N. Take the Seneca St. exit, exit number 165, on the left. Merge onto Seneca St. Turn right onto 4th Ave. Turn left onto Wall St. Turn right on Alaskan Way.

Bell Street Pier Cruise Terminal is located at 2225 Alaskan Way, just south of the Edgewater Hotel, on the waterfront. If coming by car, take the Mercer Street Exit and follow Mercer until it turns into Broad Street. Follow Broad Street to Alaskan Way. Turn left onto Alaskan Way heading south.

Parking
$12.00 per day (rates subject to change by the Port Authority)
If parking long-term, turn left on Wall Street and enter the Bell Street Parking Garage. A parking attendant will assist passengers. A shuttle van is available to transport passengers and their luggage across the street to the Terminal. Passengers can also take the sky bridge across the street to the Terminal.

TAMPA, Florida

The Seaport Street Terminal
651 Channelside Drive
Tampa, FL

http://www.tampaport.com/subpage.asp?navid=0&id=3

Directions
From the North—
* I-75 South to I-4 West OR I-275 South to I-4 East
* Take Exit 1 (Port of Tampa/Ybor City)
* Take 21st Street South
* Turn right on East Adamo Drive/Hwy 60
* East Adamo Drive/Hwy 60 will turn into Channelside Drive/13th Street
* Bear to the left and follow signs for the Florida Aquarium/Seaport Terminal
* The long-term parking lot will be on the right hand side of the street

From the South—
* I-75 North
* Take Crosstown Expressway West (toward Tampa)
* Take 22nd Street North Exit (Port of Tampa/Ybor City)
* Take 22nd Street North
* Turn left on East Adamo Drive/Hwy 60
* East Adamo Drive/Hwy 60 will turn into Channelside Drive/13th Street
* Bear to the left and follow signs for the Florida Aquarium/Seaport Terminal
* The long-term parking lot will be on the right hand side of the street

From the East—
* I-4 West
* Take Exit 1 (Port of Tampa/Ybor City)
* Take 21st Street South
* Turn right on East Adamo Drive/Hwy 60 * East Adamo Drive/Hwy 60 will turn into Channelside Drive/13th Street
* Bear to the left and follow signs for the Florida Aquarium/Seaport Terminal
* The long-term parking lot will be on the right hand side of the street

From the West/Tampa International Airport—
* I-275 North (stay in right lane)
* Take I-4 East
* Take Exit 1 (Port of Tampa/Ybor City)
* Take 21st Street South
* Turn right on East Adamo Drive/Hwy 60
* East Adamo Drive/Hwy 60 will turn into Channelside Drive/13th Street
* Bear to the left and follow signs for the Florida Aquarium/Seaport Terminal
* The long-term parking lot will be on the right hand side of the street

Parking
$10.00 per day (rates subject to change by the Port Authority)
* Covered parking garage
* No advance reservations required
* RVs will be charged per space

Reflections

A Return to Elegance:
The Story of Crystal Symphony

Crystal Cruises proudly welcomes you aboard the luxurious Crystal Symphony.

Crystal Symphony was commissioned in December 1992 and the contract was signed on March 2, 1993. Just over two years later, on April 18, 1995, the 50,202 ton Crystal Symphony sailed out of her birthplace, the Kværner Masa Yard in Turku, Finland. The design team for Crystal Symphony was headed by noted ship designer, Robert Tillberg, of Sweden.

What does a dream like Crystal Symphony cost? Over 250 million dollars in 1995. The mighty vessel is 781 feet in length (238m) and 98.5 feet wide (30m). The draft is 24.9 feet (7.6m). Crystal Symphony has a cruising speed of 22 knots and a maximum speed of 23 knots. The ship is propelled by two electric motors powered by six diesel engines with an output of 53,000 horsepower. With a capacity of 940 guests and a crew of 545, Crystal

Symphony maintains Crystal Cruises' mark of excellence with one of the best guest to crew ratios in cruise industry.

Crystal Deck 5

On Crystal Deck 5, the Crystal Cove and Crystal Plaza give an open and elegant feeling. Crystal Symphony features a two-story atrium with its beautiful stained glass dome, a splendid waterfall and comfortable Crystal Cove piano bar and lobby area, refurbished during dry-dock in November, 2001.

The semi-spiral staircase descends to the Crystal Deck 5 Crystal Plaza area, including the lobby, Reception Desk, Concierge, Shore Excursions, Crystal Society Hostess and Cruise Sales Consultant Desks, as well as the entrance to the magnificent Crystal Dining Room which offers distinctive international cuisine and a world-renowned wine list. Forward of the Crystal Plaza lobby area on the starboard (right) side is the expanded Medical Center, featuring the latest medical equipment and facilities.

Entertainment, Tiffany Deck 6

The main entertainment deck on Crystal Symphony is Tiffany Deck 6. The midship Starlite

Crystal Plaza, the elegant atrium and Crystal Cove

continued...

Important Notices

Asia Café

 Enjoy a sumptuous lunch time buffet of Asian-inspired cuisine today at our Asia Café around the Neptune Pool, Lido Deck 11 from 12 Noon to 1:30pm.

Dardanelles

We are scheduled to pick up the Pilot this afternoon at 3:00pm for our transit through the Dardanelles. Professor Bulent Atalay will provide narration over the public address system.

Satellite Reception

All electronic communication to and from the ship is via satellite. Interruptions in satellite reception can occur at any time without notice. While we regret this, and apologize for any inconvenience it may cause, Crystal Cruises cannot guarantee that communication connections for telephone, television, Internet, e-mail or fax will be available at all times in all areas of the world. We expect that our internet connection may experience extended outages due to our course on Friday, July 28, en route to Istanbul, Turkey.

Special Presentation: *Gallipoli*

The Gallipoli Campaign is one of the fiercest and most controversial battles of World War I. This documentary was produced in six years in seven different countries and is narrated by Jeremy Irons with Sam Neill. *Gallipoli* is the story of ordinary men who were forced by history to do extraordinary things. Shown today on Stateroom TV Channel 33 at 6:00am, 8:00am, 10:00am, 12 Noon, 2:00pm & 4:00pm.

...from previous page

Club offers a circular design with spacious dance floor and bandstand. The elegant club also features occasional cabaret performances.

The Galaxy Lounge, all the way forward on Tiffany Deck 6, is a 463-seat showroom sloped around a spacious hydraulic stage to accommodate Crystal Cruises' spectacular, award-winning production shows, world-class guest entertainers, variety acts and big-band dancing.

The Library on Tiffany Deck 6 Midship offers over 1,400 books and a wide selection of movies on DVD plus audio books which can be checked out daily.

Computer University@Sea gives free classes and allows guests to stay in touch electronically with homes and offices. Next door, Bridge players can enjoy the spacious and well-lighted Bridge Lounge, with comfortable tables for duplicate and rubber games. Daily Bridge instruction is offered on days at sea, with no-host Bridge games played every afternoon.

The Avenue of the Stars shopping arcade has three specialty shops around the Tiffany Deck 6 atrium: Apropos features designer apparel and accessories for both ladies and gentlemen, Facets offers fine jewelry and collectibles, and Captain's Choice displays exclusive Crystal Symphony logo apparel, gifts and sundries.

The Crystal Photo Shop displays the many pictures taken by our professional onboard photo team; it is on Tiffany Deck 6 Aft, Starboard side.

The popular Avenue Saloon, Connoisseur Club and The Bistro are also located on Tiffany Deck 6. The cozy Avenue Saloon is a comfortable meeting place before and after dinner, where night owls enjoy the piano bar entertainment in a warm ambiance. The adjacent Connoisseur Club offers a fine selection of international cigars, cognac, port wines and martinis. The Bistro serves international coffees and teas,

daytime snacks and a selection of wines by the glass.

The Hollywood Theatre shows recent-release movies and features a special audio device system for the hearing impaired.

Our new Crystal Casino has four blackjack tables, plus roulette, craps, three-card poker and mini-Baccarat. The casino also has 115 slot machines including bar poker and slant-top poker machines for your gaming pleasure.

Our alternative restaurants, Jade Garden and Prego, are both located on the port side of Tiffany Deck 6 Aft. Jade Garden features fine Asian cuisine in an elegant atmosphere. Prego offers delicious Italian fare in a Venetian ambience. The restaurants have separate entrances and breathtaking views of the ocean.

A new concept in wining and dining has been introduced on Crystal Symphony. The Vintage Room, located between the Starlite Club and Jade Garden on the port side of Tiffany Deck 6 Aft, was created to promote wine education and the vast range of fine wine selections offered on board.

In addition to occasional daytime wine tastings and discussions in this beautiful room, guests may partake in a variety of wine "themed" dinners on any evening of their choice during the cruise.

Promenade Deck 7

The full outside Promenade Deck 7 of Crystal Symphony has been designed for walking and jogging enthusiasts; 3.7 laps around the Promenade deck equals one mile.

Lido Deck 11

On Lido Deck 11, Crystal Symphony features two swimming pools, each with its own Jacuzzi* and a large deck ideal for suntanning. The Seahorse Pool is the outdoor lap pool, and Neptune Pool is an indoor/outdoor facility under a retractable magradome.

The Lido Café and Gardens is our casual dining area for breakfast and lunch. The aft dining area of the Lido Café and

Gardens has a canopy so guests can enjoy the shade while dining outside. The outdoor Trident Bar and Grill, near the Neptune Pool, serves hot dogs, hamburgers, pizza and sandwiches; there is also a full bar and the adjoining ice cream bar. The Trident Grill also offers a Late-Risers Breakfast, plus casual dining on selected evenings.

With its panoramic view and comfortable ambiance, the Palm Court is the ideal place for quiet relaxation during the day, afternoon tea service, intimate classical concerts, plus cocktails and after-dinner drinks in the evening.

Lido Deck 11's youth activities center includes the Fantasia children's playroom plus Waves teen center and video arcade.

Sun Deck 12

A completely reconstructed and enlarged Crystal Spa & Salon with sweeping ocean views completes the luxury line's fleetwide spa expansion initiative. Following the design principles of Feng Shui, the ancient practice of balance and harmony, the new facility features eight new treatment rooms (expanded from six), a new relaxation area, a private canopied teak sundeck, a new state-of-the-art steam shower and sauna area. Other highlights include custom-designed manicure/pedicure areas with sunken foot bowls, ideal for the "Sole Delight Foot Ritual" with warmed aromatherapy oils and massage prior to a full pedicure. Luxurious new dry float bed suite, appropriate for singles or couples, contain a sensory bed to create a feeling of weightlessness, ideal for "Aroma Spa" and other treatments.

The enlarged Fitness Center redefines existing space and boasts a separate room for the line's complimentary yoga, Pilates, aerobic and personal training instruction, and an expanded gym with state-of-the-art fitness equipment featuring cardio theater TV, LifeFitness treadmills, cross trainers, recumbent and upright life cycles, all with heart rate
continued...

Crystal Symphony's Commander Captain Egil Giske

Crystal Symphony's Commander, Captain Egil Giske, was born and raised in Norway's central fjord country on a small island located on the west coast called Valderøy, with a population of about 3,000. Appropriately, this island is part of the Giske Community. The more familiar city to Valderøy is Aalesund, where cruise ships pick up their pilot to sail to the Geiranger Fjord.

"I started working on a fishing boat that sailed to Newfoundland and Labrador," tells the Captain of his early years. He also spent two years working on the local ferries. It didn't take long before he was "hooked" on sea life, and, after he served his military service in Norway, he moved on to working on cargo ships as an ordinary seaman.

Navigation school followed from 1982 to 1983, which he attended in Aalesund. He returned to sea as Second Officer and then First Officer on cargo ships until he began his career on cruise ships, serving as Navigation Officer on Sea Goddess.

He soon transferred to Windstar Cruises as a Navigation Officer. His desire to progress in a life at sea took him to Captain's college in Aalesund from 1990 to 1991 where he gained his Captain's license. Returning to Windstar Cruises, he served as Chief Officer until 1992 when he joined a cargo ship in the same capacity that journeyed from West Africa to the United States.

In 1994 he joined Crystal Cruises as First Officer Senior and Safety Officer. Egil Giske became a Captain in 1995, and joined Seabourn Cruise Line as full-time Captain in 1996. The new millennium fortunately brought Captain Giske back to Crystal Cruises as Captain of the former Crystal Harmony until she was taken out of service in the fall of 2005.

Most vacations find Captain Giske in Norway visiting family and friends. Captain Giske's children include an 21-year-old son and a daughter who is 18. His son enjoys playing soccer, and his daughter enjoys sports as well. A healthy outdoor life-style seems to run in the family. Captain Giske's hobbies include sports, fishing and, of course, sailing.

"There are so many wonderful and interesting places to cruise that it is hard to select a favorite." One of Captain Giske's most memorable highlights was his first time as Captain sailing around Cape Horn. He also enjoys the city of Buenos Aires as a port of call for its food (the steak!), the tango shows and the people. As with all Norwegian captains, he also looks forward to cruising the Norwegian Fjords.

Captain Giske has served Crystal Cruises admirably, and we look forward to many years of happy sailing with such a young and talented Captain at the helm of Crystal Symphony.

Return to the Orient

We still have room! Don't miss this exciting season on Crystal Symphony's 2007 itinerary. In 2007, Crystal Symphony arrives in Asia at the end of March and will explore this exotic destination during four leisurely cruises. Starting in the cosmopolitan city of Hong Kong, the first cruise includes Taipei, Kagoshima and Shanghai as highlights and ends in a 3-night post-cruise land program in Beijing. The next cruise starts with a 3-night pre-cruise program and retraces Symphony's route back to Hong Kong with overnight stays in Shanghai, Osaka and Hong Kong. The third, slightly shorter 11-day cruise starts in Hong Kong and touches on well-loved Asian capitals such as Ho Chi Minh (also the gateway to Cambodia for trips to Angkor), Bangkok and Singapore. These stops are overnight calls so as to allow maximum enjoyment and sightseeing opportunities. The final cruise allows guests more amazing shore excursion & overland trip opportunities, some in rarely visited cruise ports, as Crystal Symphony heads North West towards India and Dubai. She will call at the beach paradise of Phuket in Thailand and then a 3-day call to the unspoiled country of Myanmar, formerly known as Burma. Two ports in India, Cochin and Mumbai, add a little spice to the itinerary before the cruise concludes with an overnight call to Dubai, a city some call the city of the future.

Don't be sorry that you've missed this perfect opportunity to explore these exotic destinations from the luxury of a Crystal vessel

Please see your Cruise Sales Consultant Randal for more details. His hours are listed on the back page of *Reflections*.

Special Interest Lecturer
Bulent Atalay

Bulent Atalay was born in Ankara, Turkey, and now resides in Virginia. The *Washington Post, Smithsonian Magazine*, NPR and PBS have all characterized him as a true "Renaissance Man, an artist, an archaeologist and a scientist." His grand-

father was a military officer who survived the horrific eight-month Battle at Gallipoli in WWI, only to be killed fighting against Lawrence of Arabia 1916. His father was a Turkish diplomat, a military attaché, who had successive assignments to London, Paris and Washington. Atalay received an early classical education attending primary and secondary schools at Eton in England and St. Andrew's School in Delaware. The latter institution, where

he served for a dozen years as a member of the Board of Trustees, was the site of the 1989 Robin Williams film, *Dead Poet's Society*. Atalay went into physics by accident when a secretary in the admissions office at Georgetown University read his intended career as 'physicist' instead of 'physician,' and he found he had latent interests in physics.

In physics, Dr. Atalay's academic work – BS, MS, MA, PhD and postdoctoral studies – have taken place at a number of universities, including Georgetown, Princeton, University of California at Berkeley and Oxford University. He has been a member of the Department of Theoretical Physics at the University of Oxford and a member of the Institute for Advanced Study in Princeton, where Einstein spent his last 25 years. He is currently a professor of physics at the University of Mary Washington and adjunct professor at the University of Virginia.

In art, Professor Atalay's one-man exhibits include exhibitions in Europe and the United States. His lithographs were published previously in *Lands of Washington: Impressions in Ink*, (two volumes), 1972; and *Oxford and the English Countryside: Impressions in Ink*, 1974, both by Eton House (and no longer in print). The books can be found in the permanent collections of Buckingham Palace, the White House and the Smithsonian.

His physics lectures have taken him around the world, as have his cultural enrichment lectures. On cruises his lecture topics have spanned art, archaeology and astrophysics. "I have not been able to get off the A's," he says. On board this cruise, Bulent will give three lectures: (1) "Nature, Numbers, Greek Temples and the Mona Lisa;" (2) "Math and the Mona Lisa: the Art and Science of Leonardo da Vinci;" (3) "Galileo and his Battle for the Heavens. The second echoes the title of his highly acclaimed book published by Smithsonian Books, now in its eighth printing, and published in English as well as in seven foreign languages. The book is available in Captain's Choice gift shop. Bulent will be available to sign copies of the book in The Bistro following his lecture.

Bulent presents his first lecture this afternoon at 1:30pm in the Starlite Club.

Crystal Visions Enrichment Program

Crystal Cruises' unique enrichment programs always include at least two expert speakers to enhance our guests' enjoyment and education on board. A prominent historian, anthropologist or similar expert on the itinerary area is always on hand to share expertise and fascinating information about the ports or global areas visited on the cruise. In addition, another renowned expert in a specific field of interest offers talks to increase guests' awareness of the wonderful world around them.

Our award-winning enrichment program also always includes instruction in Bridge, dancing and computers, and on selected sailings, experts are also invited to share their knowledge in the fields of golf, arts and crafts, yoga, health and fitness, the culinary arts, wine tasting, music, opera, the fine arts, literature and the performing arts.

Daily *Reflections* gives complete schedules and biographical information about our excellent Crystal Visions enrichment speakers and instructors.

Captain Egil Giske and the Crystal Family wish a...

Happy Birthday to:
Mr. Manuel Carrera Jr.
Mr. Seth Cohen
Mr. William Cullings
Mr. David Ganz
Mrs. Kathleen Ganz
Mrs. Suzanne Hayes Lloyd
Ms. Jo Ann Malone
Mr. Lewis Papera
Mstr. Martin Smith

Happy Anniversary to:
Mr. & Mrs. Weistock

Best Wishes!

Win a Free Cruise at Crystal Casino

CRYSTAL CASINO

Would you like to have an additional opportunity to sail with Crystal Cruises – for free? Take a chance, court Lady Luck and help celebrate the launch of our very own casino brand, Crystal Casino. In addition to "christening" Crystal Casino, you just might win the much-coveted grand prize – a free cruise on one of our beautifully-appointed ships.

This special contest commemorates the transfer of the casino operations from Caesars Palace to Crystal Cruises. But, only the name has changed – we have retained 100% of the casino managers and 80% of the current casino staff, thus ensuring the same quality casino experience you have come to expect from us.

What do you win?
The Grand Prize is a free cruise* (up to 11 days) onboard either Crystal Serenity or Crystal Symphony for two people in a deluxe verandah suite.

How do you become eligible for the drawing?
The contest will only run during cruises 6311 through 6327 on Crystal Serenity and cruises 6212 through 6228 on Crystal Symphony. The Grand Prize winner will be announced at the final formal night during cruise 6229 onboard Crystal Symphony (winner need not be present to win.)

There are two ways guests can qualify to enter the drawing for the free cruise:

- Any guest† who wins either a Slot Tournament or a Blackjack Tournament in our newly-launched Crystal Casino receives one entry into the free cruise drawing.
- Any guest† who plays on a slot or video poker machine and hits the top award jackpot with the maximum number of coins played receives one entry.

How will the Grand Prize winner be selected?
All entries will be collected from our two ships, Crystal Serenity and Crystal Symphony. The winning entry will be randomly drawn at the end of voyage 6229 on Dec. 4, 2006, onboard Crystal Symphony. The lucky winner will be personally notified by a Crystal Cruises executive.

Good Luck! Bon Chance! Viel Glück! Buena Suerte!
Refer to Terms and Conditions, available in the Crystal Casino, for details.

† *Guests must be 21 or older to enter gaming areas or to participate in monetary-based games of chance.*

Future Crystal Cruise?

We would like to remind you of the different ways you can save on future Crystal Cruises by starting your next Crystal cruise arrangements on board.

There is a discount just for starting your next cruise booking here on board and an additional discount for being a Crystal Society member, plus a further discount should you wish to pay for your cruise six months in advance.

Pick up a 2006 and/or 2007 Cruise Guide today, available at the Cruise Sales Consultant's desk in the Crystal Plaza, Crystal Deck 5 Midships.

Destination Lecturer
Dr. William Doonan

A specialist in architectural archaeology, Dr. William Doonan is Professor of Anthropology at Sacramento City College. He has a wealth of experience in education, fieldwork and excavation and has traveled extensively throughout the Eastern Mediterranean.

After receiving his B.A. in Anthropology from Brown University, Dr. Doonan worked as a nautical archaeologist in Bermuda and later managed the Archaeology division at the Earthwatch Institute. In 1990 he began graduate studies at Tulane University, where he focused on Mayan royalty. Currently, he is co-field director of a National Geographic Society-funded project on Moche archaeology in northern Peru, which was featured in the July 2004 issue of *National Geographic*.

William will talk with us about the great buildings and societies that dominated the Adriatic and Aegean worlds – from the early civilization of the Mycenaeans, through the Greeks, Romans, Crusaders, Ottomans and Renaissance Venetians.

Dr. William Doonan presents his first lecture today at 10:00am in the Starlite Club.

Formal Portraits

A Rare Opportunity...
It isn't every day that we dress up so elegantly – that is part of what makes this evening so special. Make the memory of this spectacular evening last by having a formal portrait taken by the ship's photographers. Portraits are not only a wonderful way to remember your cruise, they also make superb gifts for loved ones at home. **Ask for details about transforming your portrait into a beautiful texograph painting!**

◆ *Crystal Spa* ◆

Welcome to the Crystal Spa

It is our pleasure to welcome you to the Crystal Symphony Spa and Fitness Center. Please feel free to ask any questions, and we will be more than happy to assist you with your workout regime, your fitness goals and helping you achieve a successful fitness experience on board.

Fitness Schedule

The schedule of fitness classes and seminars offered throughout the cruise can be found in the Fitness Center in the Crystal Spa, Sun Deck 12, Aft. Fitness class times and locations are also listed daily in *Reflections*. Please feel free to stop in at the Crystal Spa and pick up a copy for yourself, which you can take with you. While there, don't hesitate to introduce yourself to the staff of the Crystal Spa & Salon.

Spa Services

The Crystal Spa offers a wide range of services including several complimentary classes to get your day off to a great start, or to work up an appetite before dinner. Take advantage of personalized treatments, including one-on-one personal training or Pilates Reformer Training, starting at $100.

Whatever your fitness goals – whether continuing your current program, embarking on a new program, or just trying out the facilities on board – we can accommodate all of your needs. It is our pleasure to be at your service.

 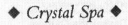 Personal Training Package

Build Muscle

Are these part of your exercise routine?
Ask the Fitness Director Dean to put together a program for you.

Blitz Your Belly

Strengthen your abdominal muscles and improve poor posture with an individually tailored training program.

Ask Fitness Director Dean about our complete cruise package.

Crystal Spa

Shipboard credits may be used on all Spa and Salon Services.
For more information, please call 3875 or visit the Spa on Sun Deck 12 Aft

Keeping Our World Crystal Clean

What standards does Crystal Cruises follow to protect the environment?

 Crystal Cruises is dedicated to preserving the marine environment and oceans upon which our ships sail. The environmental standards that apply to our industry are stringent and comprehensive. Through the International Maritime Organization (IMO), the United States and other maritime nations have developed consistent and uniform international standards that apply to all vessels engaged in international commerce. These standards include: The International Convention for the Safety and Life at Sea (SOLAS), the International Marine Pollution Convention (MARPOL) and the International Standards for Training, Certification and Watchkeeping for Seafarers (STCW). We are also obliged to follow all applicable laws and regulations in each country our ships visit. This especially applies to handling of garbage and hazardous wastes that are landed ashore for disposal. In addition, Crystal Cruises is a member of the International Council of Cruises Lines (ICCL), which has established its own guidelines that exceed the international IMO requirements which members have agreed to follow. Crystal has also implemented a voluntary Environmental Management System (EMS) that was audited and certified in February 2004 to meet the international standard ISO 14001 for Environmental Management Systems.

Daytime Activities

Good Morning

6:00am – 12 Noon	"The Morning Show" with your hosts Cruise Director Paul McFarland and		
	Crystal Society Hostess Megan Mavor.	TV Channel 27	
8:00am ★	Morning Walk on Water with Sports Director Chris. Meet your fellow walkers on the...	Promenade Deck Aft	7
6:00am – 6:30am ★	Fitness Class: *Stretch for Success* with Fitness Director Dean.	Palm Court	11
8:30am	Catholic Mass is celebrated by Father Ken Deasy.	Hollywood Theatre	6
6:30am – 9:00am ★	Fitness Class: *Stretch for Success* with Fitness Director Dean.	Palm Court	11
9:00am	Captain's Update. The latest weather and navigation information.	PA System & Ch. 53	
9:00am – 10:00am ★	Passport to Music, Class A, presented by Yamaha & Crystal Cruises. Gloria Lelter		
	teaches an innovative and fun course of piano instruction on Yamaha's newest		
	portable grand keyboards. *(Space is limited; please register in the Library)*	Bridge Lounge	6
10:00am	Paddle Tennis Open-Play with Sports Director Chris. *(weather permitting)*	Wimbledon Court	12
10:00am ★	TaylorMade Golf Clinic with PGA Golf Pro Gene Miranda.	Golf Net	12
10:00am	Crystal Visions Enrichment Lecture. Destination Lecturer Dr. William Doonan presents		
	"Commerce, Constantinople & Crusades – A Curious Tale of Faith & Warfare in Turkey."		
	(Rebroadcast on TV Channel 32 from 12 Noon to 6.00pm.)	Starlite Club	6
10:00am	Beauty Seminar: *Teeth Whitening.* Learn how to get a whiter, brighter smile		
	with Teeth Whitening Specialist Jasmine.	Palm Court	11
10:00am – 10:45am ★	Berlitz Conversational Spanish, Class A, with Rosario Mercado.		
	(Space is limited; please register in the Library)	Hollywood Theatre	6
10:30am – 11:15am	Bridge For Beginners with Instructors Robert and Anne Lurie.	Bridge Lounge	6
10:30am – 11:15am	Napkin Folding Class with Activities Hostess Mayumi.	Lido Café, port side	11
11:00am – 12 Noon	Free Gaming Instruction is available from the friendly staff in the...	Crystal Casino	6
11:15am	Jackpot Bingo with the Entertainment Staff. *(Cards on sale at 11:00am)*	Starlite Club	6
11:30am	Service Club Meeting. Lions, Masons, Rotary, Kiwanis, etc. meet with Carlo	Palm Court	11
11:30am – 12:15pm	Intermediate Bridge Lecture with Instructors Robert and Anne Lurie.	Bridge Lounge	6
11:30am – 12:30pm	Scott Mitchel plays the Crystal Piano for your midday cocktail pleasure	Crystal Cove	5

★ Indicates Creative Learning Institute Activity

Daytime Activities

Good Afternoon

Time	Activity	Location	
12 Noon	**Team Trivia** hosted by Paul from the Entertainment Staff.	Palm Court	11
12:30pm – 1:30pm	**Sundrenched Sounds** with Music Vision. *(weather permitting)*	Seahorse Pool	11
1:30pm	**Crystal Visions Enrichment Lecture.** Special Interest Lecturer Bulent Atalay presents "Nature, Numbers, Greek Temples and the Mona Lisa." *(Rebroadcast on TV Channel 32 from 6:00pm 12 Midnight.)*	Starlite Club	6
2:00pm	**Table Tennis Open-Play** with Sports Director Chris *(weather permitting).*	Horizon Deck Aft	8
2:00pm	**Free Slot Tournament.** You may register from 10:00am until the tournament starts.	Crystal Casino	6
2:00pm	**Fitness Seminar: *Detox for Weight Loss*** with Body Specialist Anne.	Fitness Center	12
2:00pm – 2:45pm	**Needlepoint Kit Hand-Out** with Activities Hostess Mayumi.	Palm Court, starboard	11
2:00pm – 4:00pm	**Duplicate and Social Bridge** with Instructors Robert and Anne Lurie.	Bridge Lounge	6
2:15pm – 3:00pm ★	**CU@Sea Class: *Introductory Computing*** with Instructor Stan Leja. *(space is limited; pre-registration required)*	The Studio	6
2:30pm	**Complimentary Dance Class** with Instructors Paul and Cheryl in the . .	Starlite Club	6
2:30pm ★	**TaylorMade Golf Clinic** with PGA Golf Pro Gene Miranda.	Golf Net	12
2:30pm	**Movie: *Take The Lead.*** When a former professional dancer (Antonio Banderas) offers his skills to the New York public school system, his traditional methods clash with his students' hip-hop sensibilities. But by combining the two techniques – and learning to work together – the class creates a style uniquely their own. Rated PG-13; 1:57.	Hollywood Theatre	6
3:00pm	**Paddle Tennis Open-Play** with Sports Director Chris *(weather permitting).*	Wimbledon Court	12
3:15pm – 4:00pm ★	**CU@Sea Class: *Basic Word Processing*** with Instructor Stan Leja. *(space is limited; pre-registration required)*	The Studio	6
4:00pm – 4:45pm Preview 3:30pm	**Champagne Art Auction!** Fun, fast and frenzied, enjoy 40-80% off land prices on artists from Dali, Rockwell, Max, Erte along with modern day favorites, Alexandra Nechita, Pino, Behrens, Deniz, sports & animation. All attendees have the chance to win $1,000 worth of art!	Starlite Club	6
4:00pm – 5:00pm	**English Colonial Tea Time** serenaded by **The Crystal Trio.**	Palm Court	11
4:30pm	**Friends of Bill W.** meet in...	Lido Café, starboard	11
4:30pm – 5:15pm ★	**Berlitz Conversational Spanish, Class B,** with Rosario Mercado. *(Space is limited; please register in the Library)*	Hollywood Theatre	6
5:00pm	**The *Five O'Clock Funnies* with Paul.** Classic comedy plus the quiz – what a deal!	Live at 5 on Channel 27	
5:00pm ★	**Afternoon Walk on Water** with Sports Director Chris. Meet your fellow walkers on the...	Promenade Deck Aft	7
5:00pm – 5:30pm ★	**Fitness Class: *Pathway to Yoga*** with Fitness Director Dean *(limited space available)*	Fitness Center	12
5:00pm – 6:00pm ★	**Passport to Music, Class B,** presented by Yamaha & Crystal Cruises. Gloria Leiter teaches an innovative and fun course of piano instruction on Yamaha's newest portable grand keyboards. *(Space is limited; please register in the Library)*	Bridge Lounge	6
5:30pm – 6:00pm ★	**Fitness Class: *Pathway to Yoga*** with Fitness Director Dean *(limited space available)*	Fitness Center	12
6:00pm	**Sabbath Eve Service.** Any guest wishing to conduct this service is asked to contact the Reception Desk.	Hollywood Theatre	6

★ Indicates Creative Learning Institute Activity

Evening Entertainment

Tonight's Dress Code throughout the ship for the entire evening: **FORMAL**
Ladies: Full-length evening gown or party dress
Gentlemen: Tuxedo or dark business suit

Good Evening

6:00pm (Main Seating)	**All guests are cordially invited to the Captain's Welcome Reception.**		
& 8:15pm (Late Seating)	The Commander of Crystal Symphony, Captain Egil Giske, officially welcomes you and introduces his Senior Officers. (While the Captain is very pleased to meet all of you, he and the other staff receiving you will refrain from shaking hands in order to provide the most effective preventative sanitary measures.) Enjoy complimentary cocktails and dancing in the...	Starlite Club	6

6:00pm – 6:45pm &	**Enjoy complimentary pre-dinner cocktails**		
8:15pm – 9:00pm	in the Starlite Club and Avenue Saloon.		
6:00pm – 6:45pm &	**Charlie Shaffer** plays for cocktails before dinner.		
8:15pm – 9:00pm	Join him in our intimate club.	Avenue Saloon	6
5:45pm – 6:45pm &	**Scott Mitchel** plays for cocktails before dinner.		
8:00pm – 9:00pm	Enjoy his stylings on the Crystal piano.	Crystal Cove	5
7:00pm, 9:00pm	**Movie: _Lassie._** Enjoy this modern remake of the 1950's classic. Starring Peter O'Toole,		
& 11:00pm	Samantha Morton and John Lynch. Rated PG; 1:39.	Hollywood Theatre	6
9:30pm – 12:30am	**Charlie Shaffer** entertains at the piano. Join him in our lively piano bar!	Avenue Saloon	6
9:30pm – 1:00am	**Music Vision** plays for your dancing pleasure. Join the Ambassador Hosts.	Palm Court	11
10:00pm – 11:00pm	**Scott Mitchel** plays for your listening pleasure. Have a drink after dinner.	Crystal Cove	5
10:30pm	**Karaoke!** Join Crystal Society Hostess Megan – be a singing star!	Starlite Club	6
Followed by...	**Disco!** D.J. William spins your favorite disco music on the dance floor.	Starlite Club	6

7:15pm (Pre-Dinner Show for Late Seating Guests) &
9:00pm (After-Dinner Show for Main Seating Guests)

Production Showtime

Crystal Cruises proudly presents our spectacular tribute to Cole Porter...

Featuring Lead Vocalists
Jennifer Simser and Cody Gay

with the Crystal Ensemble of Singers and Dancers:
Melissa Boscovich • Rachel Bury • Paul Dyke
Nicola Morton • Angi Norris • Misha Orlov
Wolfgang Schwingler • Carlo Yáñez

Accompanied by the **Galaxy Orchestra** under the direction of **Mark Oates**

Still photography is welcomed, but for the comfort of fellow guests and the safety of our performers, **please do not use flashes.**
Video/audio recording any of our performances is strictly prohibited under international copyright law. Theatrical lighting effects, including pyrotechnics, are used during the production show. **As a courtesy to fellow guests, please do not reserve seats.**

Galaxy Lounge

10:30pm	Hosted by Crystal Society		Followed by...	with D.J. William spinning
Karaoke!	Hostess Megan Mavor		**Disco!**	your favorite music!

Paul's Late Night Smile: A day without sunshine is like, night.

The Renaissance of the Classic Cocktail

In the tradition of the classic cruise ships of yesteryear, luxury specialist Crystal Cruises is celebrating a classic delight that author Barnaby Conrad III calls "a nostalgic passport to another era" – the Martini.

Crystal Cruises' sophisticated martini menu offers twelve varieties of the cocktail that has become an icon of American culture and was the favorite of such celebrated figures as Jack London, Ernest Hemingway, Franklin D. Roosevelt and Winston Churchill.

The "Crystal Martini Collection" is served in the elegant Crystal Cove, Connoisseur Club and cozy Avenue Saloon on Crystal Symphony.

In keeping with its Six-Star reputation, Crystal Cruises has adopted an elegant martini presentation. The cocktails are created from only the finest name-brand ingredients and then shaken or stirred as preferred. Presented on a silver tray, the martinis are poured into stylish Schott Zwiesel glasses from individual silver shakers and are accompanied by a dish of olives.

The Classic Martini, concocted of the purest gin, a splash of dry vermouth and finished with a perfect green olive, shares the spotlight with the Cosmopolitan, 007 Martini, Apple Martini, and eight other variations.

Drop by the Avenue Saloon, Connoisseur Club or Crystal Cove today, meet the Barkeeper, and try one of our classic Martinis.

CRYSTAL CASINO

presents...

Free Slot Tournament

Today at 2:00pm
Register from 10:00am until the start of the tournament. Maximum 30 players.

Rounds to be played are determined by the number of entrants.

PRIZES: Crystal Casino promotional items and an opportunity to win an entry to our free cruise giveaway!

FINE ART WHOLESALERS

Champagne Art Auction

Register, enjoy a complimentary glass and view our incredible collection and find out why true collectors buy at sea!

The hammer falls – enjoy 40-80% off land prices on artists from Miro, Dali, Rockwell, Max, Erte, sports and animation. Opening bid range starts at under $250 to $100,000

3:30pm Preview; 4:00pm Auction Starlite Club, Tiffany Deck 6

PERSONALITY PROFILE

Computer University @Sea Instructor
Stan Leja

Stan comes to Crystal Cruises with an impressive background. After graduating from the U.S. Military Academy, he spent almost 30 years in the Army. He has wide experience working with the global computer and satellite communications industry developing computer based systems for the Army. His academic background includes an MBA from the University of Utah, MS and Engineer Degree in Operations Research from Stanford University along with a MS in Computer Science from Texas A & M Corpus Christi. Stan is now teaching computers and information systems at the college level. An outgoing and patient personality, coupled with real enthusiasm make him very effective in helping passengers learn new skills. No computer or digital photography phobia is allowed in his classes! His love of teaching and cruising make his association with Computer University at Sea a perfect fit. After traveling and living all over the world, Stan and his wife, Mary now hang their hats in Corpus Christi, Texas.

"An Heirloom in the Making"

Crystal Symphony's Photo Shop proudly presents

Canvas Oil Portraits

This is your opportunity to capture a wonderful memory that will bring joy to you and your family for many years to come. Please contact the Photo Shop for details about Texograph and information regarding Portraits Studio times and locations.

sensors. The reconstruction increases the spa and fitness facility to almost 6,000 square feet.

Sun Deck 12 is also home for the sports fan. The Wimbledon paddle tennis court, table tennis, golf driving nets and putting green will provide hours of enjoyment.

The Staterooms

Crystal Symphony was the first luxury ship to feature private verandahs or large picture windows (not portholes) in all of its 480 outside staterooms on Decks 5, 7, 8, 9 and 10. More than 57% of the penthouses and staterooms feature large, private verandahs. The standard stateroom has been designed to offer additional space for our guests, including 15 drawers and nine feet of hanging space in the closet. Additionally, all stateroom bathrooms have two sinks, a six-foot counter and a tub/shower.

Penthouse Deck 10

In an effort to continue the most elegantly-appointed Penthouse Deck at sea, modifications have been made to the Penthouses on Deck 10, including increased drawer and closet space. Penthouse Deck 10 offers eighteen 491-square-foot Penthouse Suites and forty-four 367-square-foot Penthouses. Crystal Symphony also features two Crystal Penthouses which are approximately 982 square feet, which are among the largest, most elegantly appointed and comfortable penthouses afloat.

The completely refurbished Penthouse (category PH) and Penthouse Suite (category PS) accommodations have been redecorated with new carpeting, window treatments, custom lamps, bedspreads and new hydraulic tables for in-room dining. Italian-made fabrics in blues, peaches and lavenders, and Yamaha CD players and DVD televisions complete the refurbishment. Deluxe staterooms feature new bedspreads, carpeting and televisions with DVD and CD capability.

— Kirk Frederick

Firm and Tone Ritual

Created in France, Ionithermie combines 21st-century technology with vegetation from the sea floor.

Experience firming, toning, smoothing of the skin and inch loss after just one treatment...

50 minutes / $160
Series of 3 treatments for $399

◆ *Crystal Spa & Salon* ◆

Shipboard credits may be used on all Spa & Salon services, gifts and products. For more information, please call 3875 or visit the Spa on Sun Deck 12 Aft.

SHOPPING ON BOARD

Global Treasures

Follow your travels around the world with one of our beautiful 14k gold World Globe Pendants.

An ideal gift for the intrepid traveler.

Special Offer:
With every globe pendant purchased, receive a coupon for a free diamond, emerald, ruby or sapphire to be set in your globe.

FACETS

Reflections

 Crystal Symphony • Cruise 6219, No. 1

Wednesday, July 26, 2006
Athens/Piraeus, Greece
Sunset: 8.41pm
Evening Dress Code: Casual

Welcome Aboard Crystal Symphony

For Her "Adriatic and Aegean Sunsets" Cruise
Athens/Piraeus, Greece, to Venice, Italy
July 26 – August 7, 2006

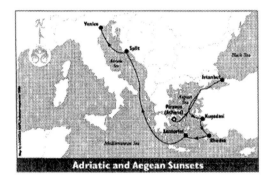

Adriatic and Aegean Sunsets

See Insert for Complete Itinerary

Also Inside:
Safety Information from Captain Egil Giske,
Important Welcome Aboard Information and
Details About This Evening's Entertainment

Important Notices

World's Best Large-Ship Cruise Line
For an 11th consecutive year,
Crystal Cruises has been voted the
"World's Best Large-Ship Cruise Line"
in *Travel + Leisure* magazine's annual
readers' survey. Crystal Cruises is the
only cruise line, resort or hotel – and
one of only three travel companies –
to have won the prestigious award
each year since the awards' inception.
Thank you for your continued support
in making Crystal Cruises #1.

**Suspension of Bridge and
Engine Room Tours**
Recent revisions to International
Regulations dictate that certain
areas of the ship are categorized as
"restricted." These areas include the
Navigation Bridge and the Engine
Room, among others. Therefore, we
regret to inform you that we are no
longer permitted to conduct tours of
these areas on board. We appreciate
your understanding.

Delayed Luggage Service
If you had any delay receiving your
luggage either at the airport or
on board, or if luggage has been
misdelivered to your room, please
contact the Concierge at the Concierge
Desk, open 1:00pm to 6:00pm,
Crystal Deck 5 Midships.

Crystal Dining Room Seating Assignments

Crystal Dining Room Maître d'Hôtel Victor Conceição is available in the Bridge Lounge, Tiffany Deck 6 Aft, from 1:30pm to 6:00pm for guests who have questions about their seating assignments.

Specialty Restaurants

Crystal Cruises is pleased to offer you the choice of two additional fine dining options aboard Crystal Symphony. Jade Garden features contemporary Asian cuisine. Prego offers modern Italian flavors. During this cruise, we invite you to join us in one or both of our specialty restaurants. Today, as it is the beginning of the cruise, we invite you to make one reservation in each of our restaurants. We ask that if you wish to make more than one reservation in each restaurant, please contact our Specialty Restaurants Maître d'Hôtel in just a few days, as we would like to give all of our guests an equal opportunity to experience our specialty restaurants during the cruise.

Jade Garden and Prego Reservations

Specialty Restaurants Maître d'Hôtel, Paolo Alario is taking reservations for these alternative dining areas today from 1:30pm to 6:00pm in Prego, Tiffany Deck 6 Aft. Please note that Jade Garden and Prego are both non-smoking restaurants.

Junior Cruisers

Children are supervised during their activities with the Junior Activities Directors, but children (ages 10 to 12) and Teens (ages 13 to 17) are free to come and go as they please, as the program is not intended to be a day-care facility. We remind all parents and guardians that, ultimately, their children are their responsibility. We kindly ask for your understanding and cooperation to ensure that guests of all ages enjoy their cruise.

Athens/Piraeus Information

Crystal Symphony is docked at the main Passenger Terminal at Atki Miaouli in Piraeus, Greece.

When going ashore, please remember to carry your Guest Identification Card, as you must show it to the officer at the gangway when reboarding the ship

From the pier to downtown Piraeus is approximately 5-10 minutes by taxi; cost around 5 Euro. From the pier to downtown Athens is approximately 20-30 minutes by taxi; cost around 15 Euro. Metered taxis are available outside the Cruise Terminal. Most drivers speak a little English.

The unit of currency is the Euro. The rate of exchange is approximately US$1 = $0.79 Euros. Due to local regulations, we are unable to host a bank on board. Money exchange offices are located in town, and many of the shops will be happy to exchange U.S. dollars for Euros.

For information about points of interest, we invite you to stop by the Shore Excursions Desk and pick up a copy of our complimentary Port Description.

Crystal Symphony remains docked overnight. Enjoy your stay in Athens.

Credit Card Imprints

For your convenience, you are welcome to leave a signed credit card imprint at the Reception Desk anytime during the cruise. Although your account is activated from the first day of the cruise, your signed credit card imprint will ensure a smooth and rapid check-out on the day of disembarkation.

Connoisseur Club

In this comfortable and elegant club – which has been called "the most beautiful room on the high seas, if not the world" – make friends and enjoy our Connoisseur Collection of cigars, cognacs, port wines, martinis, specialty coffees, single malt whiskies and fine liqueurs.

Relax in the refined elegance of this spectacular club, patterned after the fine gentlemen's smoking clubs of yesteryear.

Tiffany Deck 6 Aft

TaylorMade® Golf Program

TaylorMade is the official golf club of Crystal Cruises. Crystal is taking its golf program to a new level by offering these innovative clubs for use by its guests at the driving nets, at classes and clinics on board and as rental clubs in port. TaylorMade clubs are available for use during daylight hours at the golf driving nets on Sun Deck 12 Forward. These practice clubs include basic woods, irons, wedges and putters. If you wish to sign out any specialty clubs, please see the Sports Director in the Crystal Spa.

Rental Clubs

In addition to the clubs available at the nets, and those used by our Golf Pro for classes and clinics on selected cruises, Crystal Cruises also offers complete sets of clubs for rent to golfers who wish to take them ashore for a day of golf on a local course. Available at the Concierge Desk on a first-come, first-served basis, complete sets of men's right handed clubs and women's right handed clubs can be rented for $35 per set per day.

Our Concierges are also happy to arrange private golf outings at our various ports of call this cruise.

Hello and
Welcome Aboard
Crystal Symphony

We are extremely pleased to welcome you aboard the luxurious Crystal Symphony. All of us on board sincerely hope that the elegance and charm of our ship, along with the pleasant nature of our staff and crew, will provide you with a vacation experience unlike any other. We want you to know that every member of our staff and crew has but one goal: to ensure that you have the best cruise ever.

As you look around your stateroom, you will find a variety of amenities which are meant to make your stay more enjoyable. They include two hair dryers, a makeup mirror, a mini-refrigerator, a television with DVD player and remote control, a plush robe for use in the comfort of your room, a hydraulically-lifted coffee/dining table, plus expanded closet and drawer space for your convenience. The **Crystal Symphony Directory** is the green binder in your stateroom. This directory is designed to tell you everything you need to know about the ship and its facilities; it also includes information about how you can purchase any of our in-room amenities, should you be interested.

The key word to describe the onboard experience we offer our guests is "choices." For example, you will find that you have a wide variety of dining options aboard Crystal Symphony. Our main dining room, the **Crystal Dining Room**, is located on Crystal Deck 5. Here you will find a diverse array of first-class dishes for breakfast, lunch and dinner. The Crystal Dining Room also features one of the most extensive wine lists afloat.

Another choice is the option of enjoying your evening in one of our two specialty dinner restaurants: **Jade Garden** featuring Asian cuisine and **Prego** offering fine Italian fare. Reservations are required for these restaurants, both located on Tiffany Deck 6 Aft. Yet another option is offered on select evenings during the cruise: casual dining at the **Trident Grill**, around the Neptune Pool on Lido Deck 11; please refer to the back page of *Reflections* for days and times. If you prefer to dine in the privacy of your own stateroom, we also offer 24-hour Room Service. With all these dining choices, you will probably find that your biggest decision each day will be where to savor your meals!

Crystal Symphony also features an extensive activities program. You may choose the world-class entertainment in one of our lounges, an informative **Crystal Visions Enrichment Program** lecture featuring a noted personality or expert speaker, or an engaging class as part of our new **Creative Learning Institute**. For those who like to shop, **Avenue of the Stars** is home to three beautiful shops: **Apropos, Captain's Choice** and **Facets**. For the fitness-minded, we offer the spacious **Crystal Spa & Salon**. If Lady Luck calls to you, visit our newly launched casino – **Crystal Casino**. Or, you may choose a recent film release at our **Hollywood Theatre**. And, to remember your time on board Crystal Symphony, our professional photographers from Ocean Images take pictures at various times throughout the cruise, including formal portraits. Our daily newspaper, *Reflections*, informs you of all the activities and special events offered each day. As always, the choice is yours.

All of us on board Crystal Symphony want to make this a memorable experience for you. Should you find you need anything, please do not hesitate to ask any member of our staff. That's the spirit behind the "Crystal Attitude." If we haven't provided you with something, let us know. Like you, our friendly staff and crew have chosen the "Crystal Family." Your satisfaction is our first priority.

Again, welcome to the Crystal Age and to Crystal Symphony. Enjoy.

Please consult your green Stateroom Directory binder for complete information on the ship's dining and room service options, bars & lounges, activities and entertainment possibilities, services, general information and telephone guide.

Crystal Symphony • Wednesday, July 26, 2006

Identification/Key Card

At check-in you were issued your Guest Identification/Key Card. Be sure to carry this card with you at all times. It is necessary to have it available at the gangway every time you leave and return to the ship, as it is scanned by Crystal Symphony's security system.

Upon request, your Key Card must also be presented when making purchases on board, in order to ensure correct posting to your onboard account.

To open your stateroom door, insert the card into the door lock, front end (bow) of the ship first. Remove the card, and when the green light comes on, open the door latch.

Valuables

For your security, each stateroom and penthouse is equipped with a personal safe for small valuables that you may like to keep handy. Because you must assume full responsibility for items kept in your stateroom, we recommend that items of special value be placed in the complimentary safe deposit boxes at the Reception Desk.

Physically Challenged Guests

The alarm system throughout the ship gives audible warnings. **If you are deaf, hard of hearing, or have any other physical disability, please contact the Reception Desk** so that, in an emergency, we're aware of your special needs.

For physically challenged guests requiring Crystal Cruise Sales or Crystal Society information please call 3863 or 3870 respectively to arrange assistance.

The Vintage Room

A new concept in wining and dining has been introduced on Crystal Symphony. **The Vintage Room**, located between the Starlite Club and Jade Garden on the port side of Tiffany Deck 6 Aft, was created to promote wine education and the vast range of fine wine selections offered on board.

In addition to occasional daytime wine tastings and discussions in this beautiful room, guests may partake in a variety of wine "themed" dinners on any evening of their choice during the cruise.

By special arrangement with the Head Sommelier, private parties of up to 12 guests can be arranged so guests may enjoy this new and exclusively Crystal experience of pairing wine and food.

Guests choose an array of fine wines from our exclusive Reserve Wine List, then our Executive Chef pairs a selection of special culinary creations to enhance the qualities of each of the wines chosen. During the dinner, our expert Head Sommelier shares his knowledge of these extraordinary wines, offers complete tasting notes and explains the unique properties of the vintages with the various food courses presented.

There are special themes from which a wine connoisseur can choose, such as *A Wine Tour of Europe, Best Wines of Napa, The Italian Experience* or *New World and Old World Wine Comparisons*. Four or five wines are usually chosen, and appropriate food courses to enhance the wines are presented during the leisurely, entertaining and educational evenings in The Vintage Room.

There is a minimum charge of $1,800 for these exclusive private dinners, which includes the reserve wines and gratuity. All food on board is complimentary, so the special paired culinary preparations are included at no additional cost.

For more information or to reserve your dinner in The Vintage Room, please contact Head Sommelier Ben Van de Meutter via the Reception Desk. A votre santé!

Ship's Medical Center (Phone 9911)

Crystal Symphony's onboard medical staff consists of a doctor and two nurses. One nurse is on board at all times. Daily office hours are from 8:00am to 12 Noon and 2:00pm to 6:00pm. The doctor's consultation hours are 9:00am to 10:00am and 5:00pm to 6:00pm.

Medical attention (24 hours): dial 9911 *(let ring 5 times and then hang up; this action beeps the nurse, who will call you back immediately).* **In extreme emergency call 3333.**

The regular consultation fee is $56.00. Consultations outside the doctor's office hours and stateroom calls are subject to an additional charge. Special examinations and/or treatment procedures are charged separately, as are medications.

The Medical Center is located on Crystal Deck 5 (starboard corridor, just forward of the Reception Desk), accessible by taking the forward stairs or elevators.

Payment for Purchases on Board

For your convenience, there is a "charge only" system on board. Simply sign vouchers for all purchases and services. The charges are placed on your account and billed to you at the end of the cruise. Cash, travelers checks, American Express®, MasterCard®, VISA®, Diners Club®, Discover®, or personal checks in U.S. currency (up to $2,000 per person per cruise) are accepted for payment.

Your name and account number (5 digits = stateroom number + personal suffix) are printed on the check by the cash register. We request that each guest verify that the name and account number are correct before signing each bar bill/sales check, as the charge will be posted directly to your onboard account.

Welcome to Crystal Cruises' innovative...

Welcome to the ever-growing world of services offered by Crystal Cruises' own Computer University@Sea. Founded in 1997 aboard Crystal Symphony, Computer University@Sea has gone from being the first full-service technology center on the seven seas, to the best in a sea of imitators. Computer University@Sea offers all of the basics of a well-equipped computing facility, plus many extras you've come to expect from Crystal Cruises.

The Computer University@Sea facility provides every guest with access to top-of-the-line computer, digital imaging and desktop publishing equipment, a complete selection of productivity and leisure software and full-time connectivity to the Internet. Computer University@Sea also provides an exclusive Crystal Symphony e-mail address for those guests who either do not have access to a personal e-mail account, or who prefer to add a special touch to their correspondence with their business partners and loved ones on land.

For those guests who enjoy a more private environment in which to conduct their business, Computer University@Sea can configure personal computers or, for a nominal fee, we can provide preconfigured equipment to take advantage of the ship's network services from the privacy of your own stateroom.

In addition to the fee-based communication and publishing services that Computer University@Sea offers, you will find an abundance of free services that help make your experience on board unique to Crystal Cruises.

Computer University@Sea has worked with industry veterans over the past year developing a comprehensive curriculum all new for 2006. Classes cover topics ranging from beginning courses geared toward someone who has never had the chance to get comfortable with using a computer, to advanced application training that even veteran computer users can learn a thing or two from.

For all of the digital shutterbugs on board, Computer University@Sea's new curriculum maintains a special focus on classes on all aspects of digital imaging. And for those guests who aspire to something more than our regular curriculum, our Computer University@Sea instructor can design private lessons around your specific interests for a nominal fee. Computer University@Sea has recruited top computer industry professionals to assist you during your stay on board.

For this voyage, Computer University@Sea is pleased to welcome **Stan Leja** as our professional guest instructor. Throughout the coming days at sea he will lead classes, give lectures and make himself available to every guest who would like an extra touch of personal attention in becoming comfortable with all of the technology options at his/her disposal.

Computer University@Sea also employs a full-time staff who are available from 7:00am until 11:00pm to ensure that every one of your computer needs are met in the incomparable Crystal Cruises style. Come by Computer University@Sea, located on Tiffany Deck 6 Aft, and meet the staff to enroll in one of the many complimentary classes, to learn how to access your Crystal e-mail account and the Internet, to sign up for the Flat-Rate Internet Package or to have your computer configured for stateroom access.

Crystal Symphony • Wednesday, July 26, 2006

Crystal Cruises Creative Learning Institute

 Engaging, Enriching, Enhancing

The **Crystal Cruises Creative Learning Institute**, "CLI," brings out the best in you – by bringing you the best instruction available at sea. The Institute expands upon Crystal's commitment to enrich the body, mind and spirit by extending new opportunities for personal growth.

Featured on this cruise are:

• **Berlitz Spanish Language Classes**
• **Computer University@Sea Classes**
• **Fitness Classes**
• **Odyssey Art at Sea Classes**
• **TaylorMade Golf Classes**
• **Walk On Water**
• **Yamaha Keyboard Classes**

Each class and workshop is designed to further your knowledge in an entertaining and interactive format.

If you're interested in participating in the Yamaha keyboard or Berlitz Spanish Language classes, **you may sign up in the Library during opening hours.** Registration for CLI@Sea classes takes place at CLI@Sea, Tiffany Deck 6, throughout the duration of the cruise.

Each guest completing a designated series of classes in any of the subject areas is offered a CLI certificate at the conclusion of the cruise.

Credit Card Imprints

For your convenience, you are welcome to leave a signed credit card imprint at the Reception Desk anytime during the cruise. Although your account is activated from the first day of the cruise, your signed credit card imprint will ensure a smooth and rapid check-out on the day of disembarkation.

Daytime Activities

Welcome Aboard

10:00am – 12 Noon	**The Library is open** to check out books, DVDs and CDs.		

12 Noon	**Embarkation commences.** On behalf of Captain Egil Giske, Hotel Director Johannes Lorenz, Cruise Director Paul McFarland and the officers, staff and crew of Crystal Symphony, we welcome you aboard for this "Adriatic and Aegean Sunsets" cruise.

12 Noon – 3:00pm	**The Crystal Trio** serenades for your listening pleasure.	Crystal Cove	5
12 Noon – 8:00pm	**Salon Open House.** Find out about all the excellent treatments we have available. For this afternoon only, we are unable to take appointments by phone. Please stop by the Crystal Spa to make appointments. Spa tours available from 12 Noon to 8:00pm. Formal nights this cruise are **July 28 and 31 and August 4.**	Crystal Salon & Spa	12
1:30pm – 6:00pm & 7:30pm – 11:00pm	**The Library is open** to check out books, DVDs and CDs. Sign up for Yamaha keyboard and Berlitz Spanish classes.	Library	6
1:30pm – 11:00pm	**Computer University@Sea Open House.**	CU@Sea	6
2:00pm	**Bridge Players meet** for unhosted play.	Bridge Lounge	6
2:00pm – 8:00pm	**Paddle Tennis, Table Tennis, Shuffleboard and Quoits** are available for open-play.		
3:00pm	**Movie: *Failure to Launch*.** See synopsis on Evening Entertainment. Rated PG-13; 1:37.	Hollywood Theatre	6
3:00pm – 4:00pm	**Scott Mitchel** plays the Crystal Piano for your listening pleasure	Crystal Cove	5
3:30pm – 4:30pm	**Fitness Center Orientation.** The Fitness Director is available to answer questions regarding the fitness equipment and book private training sessions.	Fitness Center	12
3:30pm – 4:30pm	**Crystal Afternoon Tea** serenaded by **The Crystal Trio**.	Palm Court	11
4:00pm – 5:00pm	**Charlie Shaffer** plays the Crystal Piano for your listening pleasure.	Crystal Cove	5

"Adriatic and Aegean Sunsets" Cruise Itinerary

Day	Date	Port	Port Times	Dress Code	Evening Entertainment	Crystal Dining Room Dinner
Wed	July 26	Athens/Piraeus	Docked Overnight	Casual	Welcome Aboard	Dinner
Thu	July 27	Athens/Piraeus	Depart: 9:00pm	Casual	Headliner Showtime	Bon Voyage
Fri	July 28	At Sea	Cruising	Formal	*COLE!*	Captain's Welcome
Sat	July 29	Istanbul	Arrive: 8:00am	Casual	Dancing	Dinner*
Sun	July 30	Istanbul	Depart: 9:00pm	Casual	*Symphony of Nations*	Mediterranean
Mon	July 31	At Sea	Cruising	Formal	*Million Dollar Musicals*	French
Tue	Aug 1	Kusadasi	8:00am – 10:00pm	Casual	Headliner Showtime	Dinner*
Wed	Aug 2	Rhodes	8:00am – 6:00pm	Casual	*Rock Around the Clock*	'50s Dinner
Thu	Aug 3	Santorini	8:00am – 6:00pm	Casual	Headliner Showtime	Dinner
Fri	Aug 4	At Sea	Cruising	Formal	*Curtain Call*	Captain's Farewell
Sat	Aug 5	Split	8:00am – 5:00pm	Informal	Headliner Showtime	Neptune
Sun	Aug 6	Venice	Arrive: 8:00am	Casual	Farewell Show	Dinner
Mon	Aug 7	Venice	D I S E M B A R K A T I O N			

*Also Casual Poolside Dining at the Trident Grill   Itinerary, times and shows are subject to change

Evening Entertainment

Good Evening

Time	Event	Venue	Deck
6:00pm – 6:45pm &	**Music Vision** plays for your dancing pleasure.		
8:15pm – 9:00pm	Join the Ambassador Hosts.	Palm Court	11
6:00pm – 6:45pm &	**Charlie Shaffer** plays for cocktails before dinner.		
8:15pm – 9:00pm	Join him in our intimate club.	Avenue Saloon	6
6:00pm – 7:00pm &	**Scott Mitchel** plays for cocktails before dinner.		
8:00pm – 9:00pm	Enjoy his stylings on the Crystal piano.	Crystal Cove	5
6:00pm – 7:00pm	**Junior Cruisers Ages 3-12** meet your Junior Activities Director. Parents are welcome too.	Fantasia	11
7:00pm, 9:00pm	**Movie: *Failure to Launch*.** Tripp (Matthew McConaughey) has never been able to leave		
& 11:00pm	the nest for one reason or another. His desperate parents hire a professional motivator		
	(Sarah Jessica Parker) who also happens to be gorgeous. PG-13; 1:37.	Hollywood Theatre	6
7:30pm – 8:30pm	**Teens Ages 13-17 Open House.** Meet Teen Activities Directors Jennifer and David in	Waves	11
9:30pm – 12:30am	**Charlie Shaffer** entertains at the piano. Join him in our lively piano bar!	Avenue Saloon	6
9:30pm – 12:30am	**Music Vision** plays for your dancing pleasure. Join the Ambassador Hosts.	Palm Court	11
10:00pm – 11:00pm	**Scott Mitchel** plays for your listening pleasure. Have a drink after dinner.	Crystal Cove	5

7:30pm (Pre-Dinner Show for Late Seating Guests) and
9:00pm (After-Dinner Show for Main Seating Guests)

Join **Cruise Director Paul McFarland** for

WELCOME ABOARD SHOWTIME

featuring

The Crystal Ensemble of Singers and Dancers

opening with *Applause Applause*

and closing with selections from *Grand Hotel*

with a special appearance by
Dance Team

Paul Zaidman & Cheryl Smith

Accompanied by **The Galaxy Orchestra** under the direction of **Mark Oates**
Video/audio recording of this performance is strictly prohibited under international copyright
law. For the safety of our performers, please refrain from the use of flash photography.
Theatrical lighting and special effects, including strobes, smoke, haze and pyrotechnics may be
used during this production. As a courtesy to fellow guests, please do not reserve seats.

Galaxy Lounge

Paul's Late Night Smile: Dear Lord, please make me the person my dog thinks I am.

Crystal Adventures Shore Excursions

Crystal Cruises' Shore Excursions Manager Michael Braathen and his team, Gorica, Denise, Alistair and Edward, wish you a warm welcome aboard. The Shore Excursions Desk is located next to the Reception Desk in the Crystal Plaza, Crystal Deck 5 Midships, and is open today from 1:00pm to 8:00pm.

We have many exciting ports of call this cruise. Stop by and see us at the Shore Excursions Desk as we have an array of excursions available.

Crystal Adventures Channel 31
Pre-recorded presentations play continuously today, featuring tours available this cruise.

Important Information
• After booking, your Crystal Adventures Shore Excursions tickets are delivered to the mail clip outside your stateroom door.

• If you are traveling as part of a group with family and/or friends, please advise us at the time of booking.

• If making changes to tours, please bring your tickets with you to the Shore Excursions Desk.

• **Please check the top of your tour ticket for departure time and place.**

Pre-Registered Tickets
All guests who have pre-registered shore excursions will receive their tickets this evening. For details regarding the cancellation of excursions, please refer to the general conditions in your Crystal Adventures Shore Excursions book.

Needle Containers

If you administer injections for health purposes, please inform your stewardess so she can provide you with a container to insure the safe disposal of the used needles. Your use of these containers protects others.

Chief Concierge, Dale Moffitt

Dale resides in the metropolitan city of Durban, South Africa. After completing high school, Dale's desire was to pursue a career within the field of Hotel Management. The ideal opportunity presented itself in the form of a 3 year, in-house

management traineeship at the all-new Grace Hotel in Rosebank, a member of Small Luxury Hotels of the World. Theory is offered by the acclaimed Hotel School of the University of the Witwatersrand, monitored closely by the Hospitality Industries Training Board of South Africa.

Having gained firsthand experience from leading industry professionals, within all departments of the hotel and showing a passion for true five star service, Dale was appointed Restaurant Manager of the fine dining restaurant. Dale then joined the exciting world of cruising with Seabourn Cruise Lines and after completing the first contract, he knew that his career would be best served at sea.

The offer to join Crystal came just after this, which Dale had no hesitation in accepting. He began his duties at the Reception Desk and was later promoted to the Concierge Desk, where he looks forward to meeting and being of assistance to you – making your Crystal Cruise experience that extra bit special.

Concierge, Andrew Samuel

Andrew was born in Wales, United Kingdom. At an early age, he emigrated with his family to Perth, Australia, where he now has the good fortune to call home. After completing school, Andrew went on to further his education following in his father's

footsteps of engineering. He then went to Hotel School, where he discovered his niche in life. The hospitality industry allowed Andrew to travel and live in many places throughout the world, including New Zealand, South America and Europe, before joining Crystal Cruises in 2002.

During his four years with the company, Andrew has filled positions as Bar Waiter, Barkeeper, Reception Desk and now Concierge. Andrew says, "Being able to pursue a career that allows me to travel the world and assist a variety of people is an extraordinary opportunity." He looks forward to meeting you and going "the extra mile" to make your stay on board Crystal Symphony unforgettable.

Flat-Rate Internet

Computer University@Sea offers a special flat-rate package for Internet access from your stateroom or from the CU@Sea Laboratory. This special rate covers the entire cruise and is only available for purchase today and tomorrow. Please visit the friendly staff at CU@Sea for further details.

A Word About Purchasing Jewelry

Crystal Cruises is pleased to present a very special collection of jewelry from around the world showcased for you in Facets Fine Jewelry store.

We invite you to shop on board with the utmost confidence that you will receive Six-Star quality service and jewelry from renowned and trusted designers.

Our goal is to assist you in finding the perfect piece that will bring back fond memories of your Crystal cruise. We invite you to stop by during your cruise and shop at your leisure with our qualified onboard jeweler.

Crystal Cruises proudly gives you the most attentive service on the high seas.

Welcome aboard!

風水 Spa Taster

Can't decide between a massage and a facial? Try our Spa Taster:

25 minute Facial
25 minute Back Massage

50 minutes: normally $132
Special today only – $99
Offer valid for services booked and provided today only

◆ *Crystal Salon & Spa* ◆

Shipboard credits may be used on all Spa & Salon services, gifts and products. For more information, please call 3875 or visit the Spa on Sun Deck 12 Aft.

Fine Wines from Around the World

Crystal Cruises has assembled one of the most comprehensive wine lists in the industry, boasting more than 150 selections and an onboard inventory of over 25,000 bottles. The wine list, assembled under the guidance of **Head Sommelier Ben Van de Meutter**, includes selections from nearly every wine-producing region in the world.

If you have any questions regarding wine, members of our helpful wine staff are available in The Bistro to assist you during the day, and in the Crystal Dining Room at luncheon and dinner. You may also call The Bistro at extension 3847.

In order that we may provide the most efficient service, we suggest that if possible, you make your dinner wine selection at lunch or before the dinner service. Wines may be ordered in advance with the wine waiters in the Crystal Dining Room and The Bistro.

In addition, wine lists and dinner menus are available in each bar, and you can place your order with any of the barkeepers. Your stateroom stewardess also has copies of our wine lists, and would be happy to provide you with one upon request.

Corkage Fee

If you have brought your own wine with you on board, Crystal Symphony's staff is more than pleased to uncork it for you for your special event. However, if you choose to have it served in the Dining Room or in any of the public bars or lounges, a **$15.00 corkage fee** will be added to your shipboard account. If you have any questions about this service, please ask any of the bar or wine staff.

Redeeming Shipboard Spending Credits

Guests sailing with us often receive a shipboard spending credit or onboard gifts (truffles, wine, etc.) from their travel agent, from one of Crystal Cruises' travel partners such as American Express and Leading Hotels of the World, or through the Crystal Society Rewards Program.

These credits are intended to enhance your cruise experience, giving you the opportunity to enjoy additional shipboard amenities and services.

You may also sometimes receive a gift of cash credited to your shipboard account from friends, family members or your travel agent as a special "bon voyage" present. Crystal Cruises would like to clarify our policy regarding these credits and gifts.

Shipboard Spending Credits

Shipboard spending credits may be applied to any onboard purchases or services normally charged to your shipboard account. These include bar expenses (as well as wine selected with your meals), gift shop purchases, shore excursions, gratuities, laundry and dry cleaning, beauty salon or spa treatments.

Shipboard spending credits may not be redeemed for cash-related activities such as casino gaming and Bingo and may not be applied to port charges or future cruise bookings, but they may be used toward stateroom upgrades. Further, any credits not used during your cruise cannot be exchanged for cash or "held"

on your account for a future cruise (with the exception of back-to-back sailings). Any unused shipboard spending credits expire at the conclusion of your voyage.

Onboard Gifts

Gifts you receive from our travel partners during your cruise, such as chocolate truffles and wine, may not be redeemed for cash. However, should you choose to return any of these gifts, the equivalent retail value will be applied to your onboard account as a shipboard spending credit, subject to the same provisions described above. Please note that flowers may not be returned for credit, as they are perishable items. Gifts from the Crystal Society may not be redeemed for cash or credit.

Gifts of Cash Paid into Your Shipboard Account

Money paid into your shipboard account as a gift from friends, family or your travel agent is considered cash and is treated by Crystal Cruises accordingly. In addition to applying it to your shipboard purchases or future cruise bookings, you may also use it for any cash-related items such as casino gaming or Bingo.

Any unused credits from such cash gifts are refunded to you upon settlement of your shipboard account at the conclusion of your cruise.

If you have any questions about shipboard credits, please contact the Reception Desk.

Public Announcements

In an effort to respect your privacy and solitude while on board, announcements are only broadcast into your staterooms in the case of extreme urgency or emergency. Please note that all announcements can be heard on the open decks, in public lounges and on Channel 53 of your stateroom television. The Captain gives navigation and weather updates every day at sea at 9:00am and upon arrival in each port of call, shortly after the ship has been cleared by the local authorities. Periodically throughout the cruise, navigation and weather information may be given, as well as occasional program highlights and points of interest en route.

Onboard Plumbing

Although our toilet system on board is quite strong (you will notice by the flush), it is also very sensitive. In order to avoid clogging the system – which may cause the entire system to shut down – we ask that you please refrain from placing objects other than tissue (i.e. razors, sanitary items, hand towels, pantyhose, etc.) in the toilet.

USPH Advisory

Crystal Cruises consistently receives the highest scores from the United States Public Health service after inspections of our culinary operations. We are also keenly aware of our responsibility to inform our guests of specific advisories from USPH. Their most recent guidelines require us to advise you that any foods of an animal origin such as meat, eggs, fish or shellfish, which you might order not thoroughly cooked to the required minimum temperature to eliminate disease-causing organisms, can significantly increase risk to certain vulnerable consumers who eat such food in raw or under-cooked form.

Smoking Policy

At Crystal Cruises, we recognize that some of our guests smoke and others do not. Therefore, the living environment on our ships is designed to satisfy everyone. Most areas of the ship are non-smoking. There are designated smoking and non-smoking tables in most bars and lounges (except The Bistro, inside the Lido Café, the Crystal Dining Room, Prego and Jade Garden restaurants and the Galaxy Lounge, which are entirely smoke-free). Pipes and cigars are permitted only in the Connoisseur Club, and on the "open decks," except all areas of Lido Deck 11. Pipes and cigars may not be smoked in guest penthouses, staterooms, on verandahs or in corridors. Crystal Cruises kindly asks its guests to observe the non-smoking areas, which have been created for the comfort and enjoyment of everyone on board.

Visitors in our Upcoming Ports

Visitor Authorization Forms are available at the Reception Desk. Restrictions apply. We regret that no visitors are allowed on board during disembarkation day. If you wish to have visitors on board for lunch or dinner, please contact the Maitre d'Hotel. Please note that charges will apply.

Wednesday's Dining Hours

Casual Night

Breakfast

Lido Café, Lido Deck 11 Aft
Breakfast Buffet (Continental) — 6:00am – 7:00am
Breakfast Buffet — 7:00am – 9:00am

Crystal Dining Room, Crystal Deck 5 Midship
Breakfast (Open Seating) — 7:00am – 9:00am

The Bistro, Tiffany Deck 6 Midships
Late-Risers Coffee with Danish Pastries — 9:00am – 11:00am

Luncheon

Crystal Dining Room, Crystal Deck 5 Midships
Luncheon (Open Seating) — 12 Noon – 1:30pm

Ice Cream Bar, Lido Deck 11 Midships — 12 Noon – 6:00pm

Trident Grill, Lido Deck 11 Midships*
Open for hamburgers, cheeseburgers, wraps and snacks — 12 Noon – 6:00pm

The Bistro, Tiffany Deck 6 Midships
Bistro Snacks, Tarts and Pastries — 11:00am – 6:00pm

Palm Court, Lido Deck 11 Forward
Crystal Afternoon Tea — 3:30pm – 4:30pm

Dinner

Crystal Dining Room, Crystal Deck 5 Midships
Dinner (Unassigned Seating – Main Seating) — 6:45pm
(Guests on Main Seating are kindly requested to be seated within the first 15 minutes)
Dinner (Unassigned Seating – Late Seating) — 9:00pm

Jade Garden, Tiffany Deck 6 Aft (Asian Cuisine) — Closed
Prego, Tiffany Deck 6 Aft (Italian Cuisine) — 6:30pm – 10:30pm

Late Night Gourmet Snacks

Avenue Saloon and Palm Court — 11:00pm – 12 Midnight

Reservations for Jade Garden and Prego: For these specialty restaurants, we ask that you make reservations in person with the Maître d', **Paolo Alario**, today from 1:30pm to 6:00pm in Prego. On other days reservations can be made in person from 5:30pm to 6:30pm in Prego. For your convenience, you can also make a reservation by dialing 3854 anytime. Please note that both Jade Garden and Prego are non-smoking areas.

On July 29 and August 1, the Trident Grill features Casual Poolside Dining – dining in a relaxed atmosphere. No reservations are necessary.

Wednesday's Bar Hours

Avenue Saloon	5:00pm – Late
The Bistro	10:00am – 6:00pm
Crystal Casino Bar	Closed
Connoisseur Club	5:00pm – Late
Crystal Cove	10:00am – 11:30pm
Galaxy Lounge	7:00pm – 10:00pm
Palm Court	3:30pm – 12:30am
Starlite Club	Closed
Trident Bar	12 Noon – 6:00pm

Please consult your Stateroom Directory for locations of and information about all our bars and lounges.

Today's Cocktail Suggestion
• Iced Tea Cooler •

Absolut Vodka, Peach Schnapps and Calypso Mango Iced Tea... ahhhh!
The tea that refreshes.

Available throughout the day and evening in all bars and lounges.

$5.50

Printed on Recycled Paper

Avenue of the Stars Shops:
Apropos, Captain's Choice and **Facets**
The advantages of shopping on board include no sales tax and duty-free prices on many items. Closed due to Customs Regulations.

Crystal Casino, Tiffany Deck 6 Forward
Welcome to the new Crystal Casino. Our gaming regulations are governed by the Nevada State Gaming Commission. The Crystal Casino accepts only U.S. currency. Closed due to Customs Regulations.

Computer University@Sea, Tiffany Deck 6 Aft
Open 24 hours beginning at 1:30pm today.

Concierge Desk, Crystal Deck 5 Midships
Available today from 1:00pm to 6:00pm.

Cruise Sales Consultant, Crystal Deck 5
Randal Villalobos is available daily for new Crystal Cruises bookings. Please consult this space for his hours.

Crystal Society Hostess, Crystal Deck 5
Megan Mavor is available daily at her desk. Please consult this space for her hours.

Crystal Spa & Salon, Sun Deck 12 Aft
Open today 12 Noon to 8:00pm. A Hospitality Desk is available for appointments and advice in the Fitness Center, Sun Deck 12 Aft. Spa services available from 5:00pm.

Crystal Spa Fitness Center, Sun Deck 12 Aft
Open today 1:00pm to 10:00pm. Declaration forms must be signed for use of treadmills. The Fitness Director is available for complimentary consultations today.

Fine Art Avenue, Tiffany Deck 6 Aft
We look forward to seeing you at the first Fine Art Auction. Watch Reflections for details

Library, Tiffany Deck 6 Midships
Open today from 10:00am to 12 Noon, 1:30pm to 6:00pm and 7:30pm to 11:00pm. Check out books, DVDs and CDs for your enjoyment during.

Medical Center, Crystal Deck 5 Forward
Located just forward of Reception Desk on the starboard side. Open 8:00am to 12 Noon and 2:00pm to 6:00pm. **Doctor's Consultation Hours:** 9:00am to 10:00am; 5:00pm to 6:00pm. **Medical attention** (24 hours) call 9911 (let ring 3 times to page a nurse) In an extreme emergency call **3333.**

Photo Shop, Tiffany Deck 6
Photo services include processing of your film (APS and 35mm) film and camera sales and portrait sessions on all formal evenings. Closed due to Customs Regulations.

Shore Excursions Desk, Crystal Deck 5
Open from 1:00pm to 8:00pm.

Gala Welcome Dinner

Friday, September 1, 2006
Crystal Dining Room, Crystal Symphony
At Sea, en Route to Rosyth/Edinburgh, Scotland

Maître d'Hôtel **Remi Szutkiewicz**   Executive Chef **Markus Nufer**

I would like to warmly welcome you aboard Crystal Symphony. I am pleased to celebrate this Gala evening with you, and I sincerely wish you Bon Voyage and Bon Appétit.

F. Gide

Captain Egil Giske, Commander

ON THE LIGHTER SIDE

Crystal Cruises responds to today's trend toward dishes lighter in cholesterol, fat and sodium by offering these special selections:

Captain's Salad – Selected Bouquet of Fresh Garden Greens with Cherry Tomatoes, Fresh Artichokes, Cucumbers, Mushrooms, Sprouts and Crisp Celery Straw

Fillet of Grilled Fresh Baby Halibut
With Assorted Garden Vegetables, Herb Potatoes and Lemon Fillets

Refreshing Passion Fruit-Champagne Sherbet

VEGETARIAN SELECTIONS

Exotic Fruit Martini Cocktail with Champagne and Grand Marnier Liqueur

Essence of Garden Vegetables with Pumpkin Agnolotti

Sweet Potato Strudel with Cinnamon Cup Mushrooms, Grilled Parsnips and Portwine Reduction

Crunchy Vanilla Mousse with Fudge Sauce

LOW-CARB CHOICES

Clear Oxtail Soup with Wild Rice

Millionaire's Salad – Bouquet of Garden Greens, Grapefruit, Orange Segments, Palm Hearts and Thinly Sliced Mushrooms, Tossed with Raspberry-Champagne Vinaigrette, Topped with Pink-Roasted Duck Breast and Foie Gras Croutons

Yogurt Terrine with Fruit Coulis

HEAD SOMMELIER'S SUGGESTIONS

Champagne by the Glass: Louis Roederer Brut Premier, "Special Selection Crystal Cruises," Reims NV $13.00

White Wine
By the Bottle: Corton-Charlemagne, Grand Cru, Bonneau du Martray, Burgundy, France 2002 $220.00
By the Glass: Chardonnay, Chateau Montelena Winery, Napa Valley 2003 $11.00

Red Wine
By the Bottle: Cabernet Sauvignon, Silver Oak Cellars, Alexander Valley 2001 $105.00

By the Glass: Op Eximium, Weingut Gesellmann, Burgenland, Austria 2003 $10.50

For our complete selection of fine wines by the glass, please ask your Sommelier.

APPETIZERS

Napoléon of American Malosol Caviar with Traditional Condiments

Duck Liver Parfait with Dried Peach Chutney and Black Pepper Filo

Fresh Oysters on Ice with Red Wine Vinaigrette and Cocktail Sauce

Exotic Fruit Martini Cocktail with Champagne and Grand Marnier Liqueur

SOUP AND SALAD

Wild Forest Mushroom Soup "Cappuccino Style"

Essence of Oxtail with Pumpkin Agnolotti

Low-sodium soups are available upon request

Captain's Salad -- Selected Bouquet of Fresh Garden Greens with Cherry Tomatoes,
Fresh Artichokes, Cucumbers, Mushrooms, Sprouts and Crisp Celery Straw

Traditional favorite dressings available, plus today's specials:
Fat Free Honey-Lime or Low-Calorie Papaya-Ginger Dressing

SHERBET

Refreshing Raspberry-Champagne Sherbet

PASTA SPECIAL

Angel Hair Pasta with Goat Cheese and Broccoli, Topped with Pine Nuts

SALAD ENTRÉE

Millionaire's Salad – Bouquet of Garden Greens, Grapefruit, Orange Segments,
Palm Hearts and Thinly Sliced Mushrooms, Tossed with Raspberry-Champagne
Vinaigrette, Topped with Pink-Roasted Duck Breast and Foie Gras Croutons

MAIN FARES

Broiled Fresh Maine Lobster
With Melted Butter or Sauce Hollandaise, Served with Sauteed Spinach,
Baby Carrots and Truffle Mashed Potato

Broiled Chive-Crusted Fresh Halibut Fillet
Sprinkled with Bay Scallops on Carrot-Risotto, Served with Champagne Beurre Blanc

Pink Roasted Beef Tenderloin
With Port Wine Gravy, Served with Garden Vegetables and Duchess Potatoes

Mustard and Maple Syrup-Glazed Roasted Quail
With Dried Cherry and Chestnut Stuffing, Surrounded by Glazed Porcini,
Fava Beans and Sage Gravy

Upon your request, these Traditional Main Fares are also available:
Grilled New York Sirloin Steak with Baked Potato, Baby Vegetables and Mustard Hollandaise or
Plain Grilled Fresh Salmon Fillet with Herb Potatoes, Asparagus Spears and Chive Beurre Blanc

SIDE ORDERS

Truffle Mushed Potato   Sauteed Spinach   Baby Carrots

Angel Hair Pasta with Tomato Sauce   Carrot Risotto   Duchess Potatoes

Upon request, dishes are available without sauce.
Vegetables are also available steamed, without butter or salt.

Gala Welcome Dinner Dessert

Friday, September 1, 2006
Crystal Dining Room, Crystal Symphony
At Sea, en Route to Rosyth/Edinburgh, Scotland

Maître d'Hôtel **Remi Szutkiewicz**   Executive Chef **Markus Nufer**
Executive Pastry Chef **Josef Ehammer**

SWEET FINALE

"Délice au Café" – White Chocolate Coffee Cake with Raspberry Sauce

Almond-Lemon Tart with warm Blueberries and Lemon Zest Ice Cream

Crunchy Vanilla Mousse with Fudge Sauce

Sugar-Free Strawberry Tartlet with Diet Ice Cream

Low-Carb Yogurt Fruit Terrine

Truffles and Petit Fours

An Assortment of Fruit in Season

ICE CREAM, FROZEN YOGURT, SHERBET

Vanilla, Double Caramel, Blueberry Cheesecake or Chocolate Chip Ice Cream
with your choice of Mango, Strawberry or Butterscotch Topping

Freshly Frozen, Nonfat German Chocolate or Strawberry Yogurt

Refreshing Raspberry-Champagne Sherbet

SELECTIONS FROM THE CHEESE TROLLEY

Crottin de Chavignol   Camembert   Livarot   Appenzeller   Boursault
Roquefort   Served with Crackers and Biscuits

BEVERAGES

Freshly Brewed Coffee   Decaffeinated Coffee   Café Latte
Cappuccino   Espresso   Selection of International Teas

HEAD SOMMELIER'S SUGGESTIONS

Dessert Wines
By the Bottle: Château d'Yquem, Sauternes (750 ml.) 1990 $610.00

By the Glass: Kracher, Cuvée Crystal Cruises, Trockenbeerenauslese, Austria 2000 $12.00

Tonight's After-Dinner Entertainment

Production Showtime • 8:30pm & 10:45pm • Galaxy Lounge

Featuring the Crystal Ensemble of Singers and Dancers accompanied by The Galaxy Orchestra

978-0-595-43959-1
0-595-43959-4

Lightning Source UK Ltd.
Milton Keynes UK
23 December 2009

147863UK00002B/290/A